'Steve Morris is an author turned .... h a gift for entertaining writing. In this book he has mined a long-neglected gold seam of the spiritual life by championing the power of storytelling and story-listening.

'From the parables of Jesus to present day anecdotes of contemporary lives, *Our Precious Lives* blazes a trail which could show many modern churches how to grow their congregations.

'This is a literary and spiritual gem of a book which I could not recommend more strongly.'

Jonathan Aitken

'Steve Morris is a priest who's lived with his people and writes out of deep pastoral experience. He is a born storyteller and brings a wise and compassionate heart to the struggles we all face. This is a book to help us see each other more clearly, and to see the hand of the God who made us.'

Revd Mark Woods, editor and journalist

'Steve Morris is a master storyteller and in this accessible yet profound book, he uses his craft to open our eyes to the power of stories in helping us glimpse the beauty of God. With a rhythm and cadence that intertwines the ancient stories of the Bible with real-life stories of people like you and me, we are led into a sacred space. It is a refreshing and wonderful reminder of the sanctity of every life. It is in the hearing and sharing of stories that we gain insight into the incarnation and come up close and personal with the *imago dei*.'

Chine McDonald, broadcaster,
writer and Media, PR & Content Lead, Christian Aid

'Steve is a professional brand consultant, a parish priest, a devoted father and a personal friend. He is also an incredible storyteller. Stories have been the common currency of each of his roles and the common thread running through them. In this book it is clear that Steve also listens well, making space for others to tell their stories, and he delights to retell Jesus' story. I commend Steve and his writing endeavours to you.'

Krish Kandiah, founding director, Home for Good

Our Precious Lives

**Why telling and
hearing stories
can save the
church**

STEVE MORRIS

Authentic

26 25 24 23 22 21 20   7 6 5 4 3 2 1

First published 2020 by Authentic Media Limited,
PO Box 6326, Bletchley, Milton Keynes, MK1 9GG.
authenticmedia.co.uk

British Library Cataloguing in Publication Data
A catalogue record for this book is available
from the British Library.
ISBN: 978-1-78893-079-6
978-1-78893-080-2 (e-book)

Some names have been changed, and some stories are
composites of several narratives, but all come from real life.

Cover design by Luke Porter
Printed and bound by CPI Group (UK) Ltd, Croydon, CR0 4YY

Introducing the Series: Rediscovering the Heart of Faith, Life and Everything

Have you ever wondered if you are missing something? You are not alone. Church can leave us flat and faith can seem complex, difficult and hung up on propositional truth. This series is about rediscovering some of the ancient, not-so-ancient and underplayed parts of the faith – the things that really help us to live life with a sense of joy and amazement and to experience God afresh.

What is at the heart of being a Christian? Why is it something we can recommend to others? And what kind of church will help us to live out that changed life?

This series looks at some of the half-remembered aspects of the faith and the half-forgotten trinity of the church: storytelling, wonderment and mirth. The everyday stories can transform us and show us that God is in everyday life. The church that listens to those stories changes lives. When we experience the wonderment at the heart of life then we realize that being alive is a kind of miracle and we live on a planet of startling magnificence with a beautiful creator. And when we open up to mirth and merriment, we see the smiling God and the church at ease with itself, its community and others.

For my mum, Eunice, who taught me to love stories.

CONTENTS

Foreword

Steve Morris's book *Our Precious Lives* is a delight to read, and a testimony of the power of stories to capture minds and change lives. Steve has grasped the way in which the Christian story can make sense of our own stories, show us what has gone wrong, and open the door to God's life-changing grace. His moving telling of his own story is the starting point for a deep, engaging and helpful exploration of how we can make sense of our lives – and help others to do so as well.

The Christian church must never be allowed to lose sight of the fact that the gospels tell the story of Jesus Christ. Too often, the Christian faith is presented as if it is a set of doctrinal boxes to be checked, leaving our imaginations and emotions untouched. Yet Steve does more than commend the power of stories. He shows that he has mastered the art of *telling* stories – the story of his own life, the gospel story of Jesus Christ, and the story of a church that has lost sight of its roots in that story. As this book makes clear, we *can* and we *must* recover those roots. Steve shows us how it can be done.

I recently wrote a book on narrative apologetics, urging that we rediscover the power of the gospel story. As you'd expect, I've read the literature in the field. Please trust me when I tell you that Steve Morris's *Our Precious Lives* is the best manifesto I have read for Christian storytelling as apologetics. This is an eye-opening and life-changing work, that needs to be devoured and digested by pastors, apologists and evangelists. But most importantly of all, it will enrich the spiritual lives of ordinary Christians, who will gain enormously from this book as they read the Bible, and talk to their friends about their faith.

Alister McGrath
Andreas Idreos Professor of Science and Religion
Oxford University

Storytelling matters enormously because it is a story, of course, that stands at the heart of our faith and that . . . speaks to our hearts and illumines our own stories.

Frederick Buechner, Secrets in the Dark[1]

. . . all mankind is of one author, and is one volume; when one man dies, one chapter is not torn out of the book, but translated into a better language . . .

John Donne, Meditations[2]

PART ONE

Listening to Stories

1

First Word

If history were taught in the form of stories,
it would never be forgotten.

Rudyard Kipling, *The Collected Works*

I wonder what is your life whispering to you? Or perhaps it is shouting so loudly that you can't concentrate? It can be hard to escape our own stories, and we sometimes feel harried by them.

We are amazing creatures relying for our day-to-day survival on internal pumps and plumbing, scaffolding and electrics and yet we are more than gene machines.

We are created with a need to make sense of our lives and the lives of others. We are inquisitive and are beset with questions. We are full of stories, and we cannot live without them. Even with the march of evolution we have not outgrown them.

It is as if 'Once upon a time' will not let us go. It has a power over us that seems to be more than just about entertainment.

My life has been changed by stories. The stories I heard from my family helped me to see the struggles we had faced and the resilience we had shown. My school friends' and teachers' stories opened me up to new possibilities and horizons.

Stories today

Organizations have been alive to the power of stories for many decades. Management thinkers have spoken about organizational culture – or the way we do things around here – and that includes the stories an organization tells about itself. The business world knows that in many ways a company or charity or school is only as good as the story it has to tell about it itself and others tell about it.

Stories bind an organization together and give it a uniqueness – often with a founding narrative that speaks through the generations.

It isn't just organizations that understand such things. We are awash with stories. For instance, a TED Talk often begins with a personal story and that story acts as a pointer to orientate what is to come. It is as though we need a story to underpin an idea – to make it personal and to give it credence. In an age when facts are suspect, we need stories to help us to accept a truth.

Perhaps Christians have been a bit slow on the uptake when it comes to stories. This is odd because the founder of our faith tended to speak in short provocative stories. His teaching revolved around parables and the stories told about him revolved around the plot of his birth, life, death and resurrection. The New Testament reads more like a novel than a manifesto.

Given this, it is surprising that we so often reach for propositional truth to explain what we are about. Alister McGrath delicately makes the point:

> If C. S. Lewis and J. R. R. Tolkien are right in their belief that God has shaped the human mind and imagination to be receptive to stories, and that these stories are echoes or fragments of the Christian 'grand story,' a significant theological case can be made for affirming and deploying such an approach to apologetics.[1]

Our explanations of why we have the 'truth' come better as stories than simple propositions. I sometimes wonder if the large banner outside a church with a truth such as JESUS IS LORD may do more harm than good. After all, if we know nothing of the faith or the founder of it, then what are we meant to do with such a bald exclamation? The most obvious response is, 'Who says so?'

It's worth wondering what the world would be like without stories – what would our discourse and interactions consist of? A world without stories would be like a world without birdsong.

When a dictatorship begins to take power, it often begins by forbidding certain stories and books. It sometimes seems that oppressors take stories more seriously than we do. The dictators know the power of stories and they want those voices silenced.

Ray Bradbury wrote his science fiction dystopia *Fahrenheit 451*[2] in 1953. It was at the height of the McCarthy purges and assaults on free speech. Bradbury wrote his little novel on a hired typewriter. He wrote it swiftly and it has remained in print ever since.

In later years he began to distance himself from the notion that the book had a prime motive of exposing McCarthyism. Instead, he said, it was about the mind-numbing effects of the mass media.

451° Fahrenheit is the temperature needed for the paper books are printed on to burn. The novel paints a bleak picture of a society where books are burned and those who read them are killed. Books and the ideas and tales they contain are dangerous.

The book's hero, Guy Montag, is a book-burner turned book-lover.

Fahrenheit 451 still has the power to shock. It is sparsely written, but its vision of a society addicted to crass TV, zonked out on pills and where suicide is a natural response to the deadness of life seems terribly real.

It is a plea for more stories to be told, for counter-cultural stories to be welcomed and for us to get away from consumerism. It would have been a parable if it had been said 2,000 years earlier by a travelling Jewish rabbi from Nazareth.

So, this short book aims to redress the balance. It is about storytelling and how hearing about a life can open us to the wonders of God and open up ways of living out our mission, which is to love God and to love our neighbour.

A nagging voice

But as I write it, I have a nagging voice – a word of caution that I can't shake off. After all, if I want to write about the subversive power of stories, then I can't go censoring a subversive voice that has developed into an earworm.

What if stories and the art and culture that they are part of is, after all, no real defence against the darkness? Artists themselves have been aware of the seeming fragility of culture to hold back evil.

Florian Illies' charming book *1913: The Year Before the Storm*[3] shows a Europe that would have never guessed it was about to be plunged into carnage. In the year before the First World War he paints a story of the artists and cultural icons – Freud, Rilke, Joyce and others. But despite their work and their art, nothing could stop the juggernaut of war. Art is powerless to defeat evil.

One of the greatest and saddest novels about the impotence of culture is Ishiguro's *Never Let Me Go*.[4] As is often the case, the critique of culture has to be done via dystopia. In the novel we see the tragic case of a society where some humans are bred to be organ donors – and to have those organs harvested. They have no real idea of what is at stake or the cruelty that has made them what they are.

The young people who are donors are kept safely away from the sensitivities of the majority population, in special schools. In one school, the head teacher tries to prove that the donors have a cultural sense – that they are more than just organs for others. The youngsters paint.

But the denouement is as chilling as it is all in vain. The cultural value of the donors convinces no one. It is no barrier. It cannot defend them. They are disposable.

We shall have to live with this nagging voice of doubt. Is culture as we know it a product of advanced capitalism, a luxury? Are stories of ultimate importance or no importance at all?

Are stories of ultimate importance or no importance at all?

This little book is about the power of stories and it is an encouragement to the church to be the place where they are told and heard. In being that place, everything changes and we live out the truth of the incarnation that everyone matters and deserves to be heard. And that includes the lost, the lonely and the marginalized. It also includes the argumentative, the awkward and those who don't agree with your doctrine.

Interestingly, Jesus would have been changed by the stories he heard when he was growing up – from his mates, his extended family and the customers who came into the family business.

Like the rest of us, the Jesus who walked the earth was a storytelling animal. Stories would have formed him and been part of his day-to-day life – part of the fabric of who he was. Perhaps none of us can escape stories – but then, who would want to?

Study questions

1. *My life has been changed by stories. The stories I heard from my family helped me to see the struggles we had faced and the resilience we had shown. My school friends' and teachers' stories opened me up to new possibilities and horizons.*

   How has your life been changed by stories? What kind of family stories did you hear that had an impact on you? How has hearing the stories of your friends played a part in your life?

2. *It's worth wondering what the world would be like without stories – what would our discourse and interactions consist of?*

   Try to imagine what a world without stories would be like. What areas of life would it affect?

3. *Is culture as we know it a product of advanced capitalism, a luxury? Are stories of ultimate importance or no importance at all?*

   Are stories just entertainment? What is the importance of stories and culture? What part do stories play – in the Bible, in our faith and in the world around us?

Prayer

Thank you for the stories that have been part of my life. Thank you that we can tell our stories and listen to the stories of others. Please let us be open to the stories of other people. Lord, please help those who are unable to tell their stories – either because it is too difficult for them or because it is dangerous to do so.

2

I Fell in Love with Stories – And Then Forgot How to Listen

Do you see the story? Do you see anything? It seems to me I am trying to tell you a dream – making a vain attempt, because no relation of a dream can convey the dream-sensation, that commingling of absurdity, surprise, and bewilderment in a tremor of struggling revolt, that notion of being captured by the incredible which is the very essence of dreams . . .

Joseph Conrad, *Heart of Darkness*

Since I can remember, I have been hopelessly in love with stories. Maybe you are too. As a boy I always had my head in a book and then for most of my adult life I have been a writer.

As a youngster I would go to the library with my mum and read. I'd do it every afternoon after school. Reading with my mum defined our relationship – and this nurturing of her quirky, imaginative son has shaped my life.

Over the years, some of the most real people I have ever met have been in novels. Novels have influenced me and changed me and given me insights into the lives of others.

Stirring tales of quest and adventure like *Lord of the Rings*[1] got me through some tough times when I was growing up. As a teenager, Jimmy Porter in John Osborne's game-changing play *Look Back in Anger*[2] felt to me like my own twin brother. Later, magical realism swept me away, and the great American novels worked their scope, pace and magic.

I loved stories because they seemed to give *my* life shape. They allowed me to escape my current situation and they transported my imagination.

As I grew older, I began to enjoy listening to the stories other people told me about themselves. My family was alive with stories. There were grandmother's stories of a deprived and brutal childhood in London's East End, stories of the war and stories of relatives. Plus, we owned the local hardware shop in my home town of Northolt on the far outskirts of London. So we'd have a procession of people coming in and chatting to my parents with stories ranging from the funny and incredible to the poignant and tragic.

My parents always had time to listen and to make a person a cup of tea. It was part of the life of the shop. It helped that my parents did not judge those who told us their tales.

I think I knew from early on that when someone tells you the story of their life, you see them differently. You begin to see the contours and vistas of their narrative and their experience. You see the dark and light corners that make up a person.

> When someone tells you the story of their life, you see them differently.

In the New Testament it is the little autobiographical details that we learn about the disciples that helps us to see them as real people and not simply actors or mouthpieces. When we realize that Peter, the rock of the church, had his very rocky moments, we begin to warm to him. When he manages to get everything wrong on the mountain of transfiguration, we see a person rather like ourselves – able to open mouth and insert foot. When we notice that he seemed to want to be liked and that this led him into all kinds of trouble, then we see his vulnerability, and this makes us more open to what he has to say.

And then there is the most fully drawn of all the characters in the Bible – Paul. When we realize that Paul suffered terrible moments of emotional depression – real ups and downs – we see him as more than simply the person who wrote those complicated letters. And we also begin to see the sometimes complicated dynamic between him (the one-time persecutor wracked with a knowledge of what he did) and the rest of the apostles (eyewitnesses and more part of the in-crowd).

When we know the backstory, we begin to realize that other people are just as complicated as we are. This is especially true if that story is told with honesty and helps us to understand what makes the person tick, what is, and has been, important to them and how they became the person they are. How do they make sense of themselves and the chapters of their life? When we know this, then we can develop deep friendships built on mutual trust. At the very least we might be able to forgive them if they are unreasonable, grumpy or difficult.

In my ministry as a priest I began to come into contact with people's stories. Indeed, as with doctors, we are privileged to be the keepers of stories. That is what people have to offer us. People trust us with them. I quickly became aware that there are some seriously lonely people. Some people who I talk to seem to speak to no other loving souls all week. They cannot believe that things have got as bad as this.

But there was a time when I forgot to listen

I wasn't always a priest. In fact, for much of my adult life I was working in commerce. And for many years, I ran a brand agency that started out as a venture in my spare room and became something of a sensation. By some odd alchemy everything I touched seemed to turn to gold.

When I was running my brand agency, I only seemed to meet people who were buzzy and who were surrounded by equally successful friends. I was always busy and everyone I knew was busy. I lived what can only be called a gilded life. I travelled first class. I only used taxis and never took the bus. I got on planes and was a consultant around the world. I had staff and ran an organization that was successful and rather glamorous. I had travelled a long way from the anxious and timid comprehensive school boy who worked in his mum and dad's shop.

At times I had to pinch myself. But perhaps I did not pinch myself enough. I was losing contact with my roots. I was no longer the boy from Northolt – at least, I didn't feel that I was.

Looking back on those years I now see that my view of life was unrealistic and insulting to those less fortunate than myself. The stories I heard and the stories I told were shallow. And during this time, I stopped reading for pleasure. I didn't read a work of fiction for years. In spare moments I wondered where the boy who loved books had gone.

But even in those years, I was not quite lost. Not quite. Because deep in my own heart I was unhappy and restless. By the end of this period I felt trapped and desperate to find meaning. I think that most of the people I knew during this period were trapped also.

I had a moment of epiphany. I was desperate for a break, exhausted and low. My wife had been very ill and life was so tough that I did not know where to turn. We booked a holiday. It was the first holiday for eighteen months and the first break since my wife's illness. I got a call from a client on the morning before we went away. They were insistent that I go in to help them. I explained about the holiday, but that carried no weight.

At 9.30 p.m. I was in an office on my own, way outside London. I had missed my holiday. I had no way of getting home and my clients had left without telling me. I realized that in my working life, no one really cared about me and my family and that I was simply a well-paid hired hand. When I had outgrown my usefulness that would be that. I knew that life had to offer more than this.

The story of my conversion to Christianity in my early forties is for another time. The giving up of my life as an entrepreneur and businessman is for another time also. But one of the products of becoming a Christian, and later a priest, was that I began to hear the stories of those who had no one else to tell them to. My ear became tuned to a different beat. I began to see a side of the world that I had been insulated from.

Reconnecting

When I became a priest, I began to become attached to stories again. I began to think that we have to reclaim them and see them as the bedrock of the Christian Way, of a healthy society and of our own health and wellbeing.

My church is named after that great northern saint, Cuthbert. He led a revival of the faith and is known as the 'fire of the north'. His uniqueness came down to the way he would visit local settlements, most of them pagan and poor and would spend time simply sitting and listening to the stories of the families who lived there. They loved him for it. He was a good advert for the faith, and many of those he took time to listen to became Christians.

I realized that life becomes impossible when we have no one who wants to listen to our stories, or we find it hard to tell our story – because of trauma, grief or violence.

Many of the older people we have worked with at my church had stopped telling their stories because no one seemed interested. They also, I think, felt embarrassed to be left so alone. They never imagined, when they were bringing up their families, had good jobs and the world seemed full of possibility, that one day they would be surrounded by the memories of friends who had moved or died and that they would be just another elder with no one to talk to.

Baby boomers probably expected the good and sociable times to go on forever. They did not expect to be left alone.

Family members have sometimes heard all the old tales and don't want another dose of nostalgia. It is easy to lose interest in a parent's story of their youth when you've heard it countless times before.

Learning to listen to stories and to tell them has transformed my ministry and my faith. It has helped me reconnect with a part of myself that I feared I had lost.

It all began when I was new into my first role as a parish priest and when I was dragged along to a talk I didn't want to go to. I was shocked into thinking again about what I had been called to do.

Study questions

1. *Over the years, some of the most real people I have ever met have been in novels. Novels have influenced me and changed me and given me insights into the lives of others.*

   Which characters in novels and books (including the Bible) have influenced you? Why did/do they have such a powerful impact?

2. *I think I knew from early on that when someone tells you the story of their life, you see them differently. You begin to see the contours and vistas of their narrative and their experience.*

   How has hearing a person's story changed the way you think of them? How do the biographical details that we see in the Bible help us to see the characters in a more rounded way? How would you describe, for instance, a character like Paul? What do we know about his life and how might that have shaped his ministry and thoughts?

3. *Many of the older people we have worked with at my church had stopped telling their stories because no one seemed interested. They also, I think, felt embarrassed to be left so alone.*

How does this make you feel? What groups do you think find it hard to be heard? What might Jesus say about these forgotten groups?

4. *Learning to listen to stories and to tell them has transformed my ministry and my faith. It has helped me reconnect with a part of myself that I feared I had lost.*

How can listening to stories transform our faith? What stories of faith and life have you heard that have helped to strengthen your faith or helped you to see your faith a little differently?

Prayer

*Please give us opportunities to hear the stories
of those who feel left out. Help us to feel more
empathy for the struggles and difficulties of those
people we come into contact with – especially those
who we find difficult and challenging.*

3

Sunday Evening Starts the Journey

To answer before listening –
That is folly and shame.

Proverbs 18:13

As I say, some time ago I went to an evening talk at a local church. A visiting pastor had come down from Scotland to do the talk and some friends took me along. To be fair, I wasn't expecting a great deal. I probably would rather have been tucked up at home watching Sunday evening television. I had already heard a long sermon in the morning. But along I went.

As the pastor's talk unfolded, I realized that it was going to be a really significant event. I woke up and began to take notice. To understand why, we need some personal history of my own. The story I heard triggered a memory and an experience from my youth.

A family alone

My grandmother, Lily, was a Cockney. Having been bombed out during the war, she lived alone in a small flat in Mill Hill, north London. She had lost her beloved husband on the last day of the war and had been alone ever since. What made her isolation all the more real was that she was deaf. In those days she had no hearing aid, so she lip-read.

As a teenager, I would get on the bus and go to visit her. These were the days long before mobile phones, so I couldn't let her know to be expecting me. Each time I got to her flat, there she'd be, looking out of the window. Almost before I got to the door, she would be welcoming me in. She was at that window every day.

When I got inside, she'd tell me all the stories of her youth – growing up in the East End, stealing fruit from the local stall because she and her six brothers and sisters were so hungry, being sacked from working at the sweet shop because she ate more than she sold. I heard about the bomb that demolished her house. I heard about the old days in the East End and stories of my father growing up.

I lapped up the stories. In one way I absorbed the stories into my own life. Her stories of growing up began to help me make sense of my own narrative. I tell those stories to my own children and they are a glue that binds our family and always keep us grounded. We know where we come from and we take pride in the everyday life of our forebears.

But in the years that followed, when I was away at university, I began to wonder. Why was my grandmother always at that window? I could not get that worrying thought from my mind. And it struck me that it was because she was painfully lonely and had no one to talk to. The walls were closing in and if she looked out, just maybe someone might turn up to listen to her. She hoped that she might get a visitor, even though experience told her how un-likely that was.

It made me sad. But as I got older and after my grandmother had died, it began to make me angry and I wanted to do something about it. I wondered why there was no place and no one to hear my grandmother's story, and the millions of people like her, and why there was no one to tell her theirs.

Sunday night

And so, we go back to our friend, the visiting pastor.

He explained that in one of the churches where he served, things were not going so well. He was feeling isolated and the church wasn't thriving. It is so easy to hit the wall as a pastor – especially when the early excitement turns to grind and discouragement.

He had come into the role thinking that if he put in a big worship band and ran an Alpha course and all the rest, that the church would grow and disciples would flourish, but it was not so. The church was stagnant, and the faith of all concerned seemed to be low. He spent hours putting together his sermons but was losing heart.

Being a pastor is a very tough job and, when your church is in the doldrums, there are few jobs tougher. We tend to think that if we preach harder and worship louder, it might drown out the terror that our church might peter out, or our ministry fail. In the early days of my ministry here at St Cuthbert's I would sometimes get the horrible thought that one Sunday only me and the organist might turn up.

Eventually an elder took the pastor giving our Sunday evening talk to one side and explained: 'Get to know everyone's story and then you can be their pastor. Until then you are *just* a preacher.'

This was a challenging thought. Many churches tend to outsource visiting to a pastoral team – seeing the minister's role as teaching and preaching. It can be a daunting task to go around to a person's house, and many clergy are a bit shy and awkward with people. It can be hard to find the right words. It is all too easy to maintain distance with a congregation, but maintaining closeness is an altogether different proposition. It is much more challenging. And how to fit in visits when there is so much to do during the week?

He explained to us that he decided on the spot to meet every single person in his congregation and ask if they would bless him with their life story. This was a tremendous commitment but it was one he took seriously. He began making calls and booking up appointments.

It took months, but as the stories flowed, he began to realize the heroism of people's faith – how they had got through the death of a child and loved one and still clung to faith, how they overcame morning depression and still came to church regardless, and of the joys of ordinary, everyday lives. He heard about their triumphs and their families and their hopes for their children. He heard about their work and times of distress and trouble. He heard stories of how they had clung onto their faith by their fingernails. He heard stories of joy, of angelic encounters and of amazing miracles. He heard testimony of the work of the Holy Spirit and of reconciliations that never seemed possible.

Many folk described times of supernatural oppression and fear, and this surprised him. Although when he thought about it, he realized that he too had felt the same sense of impending evil and unsettledness.

He spoke to young and old, and as word got around that the pastor was good at listening, more and more volunteered for a visit. Each time, he would respectfully sit and listen and at the end would pray with people. Oddly, as the days and weeks went by, more people began turning up to church on a Sunday, and they began to bring friends and relatives. Rather than rushing off at the end of the service, people stopped to talk to the pastor and to each other. People volunteered to help out at church.

Listening to stories brought the people to life and stopped them from being a congregation and started them being the people God had given him. He began to see the people in colour rather than in black and white. They began to feel like family, and he felt welcomed into their homes and hearts.

I remember him saying to us: 'I realized that for some people just coming to church is an act of heroism.'

He explained that the listening to stories adventure had restarted his ministry. All the other things he had planned could be done, but now with more love and relevance as he was dealing with people who had entrusted something precious to him. He began to understand more what a worked-through faith looked like and he stopped judging people for sometimes missing church. If your husband can't get out of bed and your kids are struggling at school, then just on the odd Sunday your act of worship is to be at home looking after them.

The act of storytelling *was* evangelism. It was evangelism because in the telling of the stories people began to see the good news of how God had been with them and how their lives were holy in all their ordinariness.

The lives of others

There is a wonderful film about Communist East Germany called *The Lives of Others*.[1] In it, a Stasi operative is sent to listen in to the bugged apartment of some artists to see if they are falling foul of the regime. He is given the task of collecting evidence that they are enemies of the state. He sets up in a dispassionate way and expects to find these people decadent. The East German state was exceptionally buttoned-up and fearful of joy.

As he listens, he begins to catch something of the joy and struggles of those inside the flat. They are no longer targets, they are people. The operative is seduced by the reality of human experience and as he listens to the lives of others, he sees them as people and begins to see freedom in the way they live. He finds something deeply attractive in their lives. He begins to like them. He cannot betray them.

As he listens to the stories they tell and the intimate story of their lives unfold, he can no longer remain an onlooker. He begins to reflect on his own empty life and the empty politics of the state he represents.

The film is almost a metaphor for our work as the gatherers and keepers of personal histories.

When we know a person's story, we know what they are carrying. There is much scholarly debate about who first said it, but we surely all could sign up to: 'Be kind, for everyone you meet is fighting a hard battle.'[2]

Stories and renewed ministry

The story that I heard on that Sunday night took me out of my comfort zone. I decided, there and then, that I was not fit to be a priest if I did not take the time to listen to stories. I wanted to hear about *my* people's lives – the lives of everyday love and joy and pain and sadness. And in listening, to affirm that every life matters.

> I was not fit to be a priest if I did not take the time to listen to stories.

That commitment led to a ministry that had surprising effects. And since then I have spent as much time as I have preparing sermons or doing services or any other of the many tasks a parish priest has.

One thing has surprised me in my quest to be a story listener and collector – hope. People have told about the extraordinary struggles they have faced.

Losing loved ones, addictions in the family, bankruptcy, illnesses and disastrous accidents. They have told me about caring for loved ones who have lost all sense of who they are. But there has been the precious shard of hope in each of their lives. I name this hope as 'God with us'. By all external measures they should have given up, retreated to their beds and never left the house again. But they bounce back and they do not describe their lives as being a case of bleak existential hopelessness. I am sure they are doing this not just to please me. They mean it.

What if people were to say about your church that it is a place where people took time to hear their story? I think that this would be a mighty testament to the incarnational God who had time to listen himself and lived a life just like ours.

And there's another reason why stories might be important.

Stories and brain chemistry

Perhaps 'Once upon a time . . .' is more than just an invitation to entertainment.

What happens to our brains when we hear a story? Talking about the central characters in any story,

John Yorke says that *we* live through stories and 'experience the stories of others as a kind of telling of our own. When a character is in danger, *we* feel in danger. When they are happy, that happiness rubs off on us too'.[3]

Stories have a kind of witchy power. They are fundamentally attractive and we all find them hard to resist. It is telling that Jesus used stories so foundationally in his ministry – that was what the culture expected, yes, but in so many other ways he was counter-cultural.

Even if we try to avoid stories, one story at one time or another will pull us towards it and to the prospect of a different reality that we can inhabit. The pull of a reality that is different to our lived-reality is an enticement.[4]

In fact, it appears that listening to a story can actually change our brain chemistry and, ultimately, our actions. Twenty volunteers were paid to hear a story about a dying boy and his father. Before they heard the story, they took a blood test. After the story they took another blood test and this revealed raised oxytocin – the empathy chemical. What's more, half of the participants went on to donate half of their fee to the cause of the dying boy.[5]

Stories change our brain chemistry. Interestingly, if the volunteers above were given a factual Power-Point presentation on the above tale it would have no impact on their chemistry.

Perhaps one of the reasons we rely so heavily on stories to make sense of our chaotic lives and world is that our 'factual' memories are so hopeless. Even a few years after a powerful event we might all have slightly different ways of remembering it.

We live our lives in a daydream, often unable to tell the difference between fact and fiction. We are un-reliable narrators of our own lives – which is fine because it means that fiction and reality have equal worth and value and are equally at the core of us.

Study questions

1. *Eventually an elder took the pastor giving our Sunday evening talk to one side and explained: 'Get to know everyone's story and then you can be their pastor. Until then you are just a preacher.'*

   Why was this good advice? What is the difference between a preacher and a pastor? Is it possible to be both? How might spending time simply hearing the stories of others change your ministry or faith?

2. *'I realized that for some people just coming to church is an act of heroism.'*

   Discuss. Why is it hard for many people to get to church? Why might it show courage to be there? What examples can you share of everyday heroism?

3. *Stories have a kind of witchy power. They are fundamentally attractive and we all find them hard to resist.*

   What is the power of story? Why are they attractive? Why do you think Jesus used stories in his ministry rather than just telling a factual truth?

Prayer

Thank you for calling me to be a listener as well as a speaker. Thank you for the everyday heroism of people's faith – the way they still carry on even when life becomes tough. Help me to be open to listening, just as the Sunday-night pastor was. Lord, please be with those who are struggling with their faith, facing times and problems that seem insurmountable, and help us to listen and be there when we are needed.

4

The Funeral Before the Funeral

The Mole was bewitched, entranced, fascinated. By the side of the river he trotted as one trots, when very small, by the side of a man who holds one spellbound by exciting stories; and when tired at last, he sat on the bank, while the river still chattered on to him, a babbling procession of the best stories in the world, sent from the heart of the earth to be told at last to the insatiable sea.

Kenneth Grahame, *The Wind in the Willows*

As a parish priest, I became fed up with telling the amazing story of a person's life only when they died. At the end of a funeral people would come up and say they had no idea what an amazing life the person who died had. Why did we wait so long to find out? If we had known earlier, we could have honoured that life as a great testimony to God's love and creativity.

I wonder if the surprise people feel when they hear about the story of a loved one's life is symptomatic of a society that has forgotten how to listen. We are all guilty of it.

Just recently I attended a great-uncle's funeral. He died just a month before his one hundredth birthday. I learned that he was a fluent Italian-speaker. He learned Italian so that he could speak to the Italian prisoners of war he guarded. Interestingly, he did this because he felt sympathy for them. His faith was important to him, and learning a language was an expression of that faith and compassion for those who he had been fighting against. It was good to know this – it helped to make sense of his life and his faith.

I learned that George co-owned a trout lake but never fished and that he completed the *Telegraph* crossword every day right up to the end of his life.

These seemingly mundane elements made me feel closer to him and I wish I'd known about them before he died. The story also helped me to see a fuller picture of George and to be more thankful to God for the life my uncle had lived.

If we take the incarnation seriously, then seeing God at work encourages us to do the detective work. If we can hear a story then we begin to see how precious people are, how complicated they can be, and how this glorifies the Christ who himself was complicated, sometimes confusing and mysterious.

After a person's death, in the many funerals I have conducted, I have found out so many things. One person flew Spitfires but never spoke about his experiences after the war, another was an 'exotic' dancer and another scored a double century at Lord's Cricket Ground while captaining his country. The 'exotic' dancer was the primmest person at our church. The story of her times at the Raymond Revuebar were delectable and gave me fresh hope that people can have adventures, and that what we see is not always who they are. Those we share our lives with can be a great mystery.

I can't be alone in feeling a sense of wonder when I hear a life story. Such stories help me to frame my own story and help me to see that God is truly great.

It also helps me to be aware of the miracle of life. This is quite different from a formulaic testimony – a retelling of a moment of God's intervention in a life. Of course, there is a time and a place for this. If someone asks you why you believe in God, then a detailed account of your time studying French in sixth form isn't really what's required. No, hearing the whole thing, hearing the seemingly unconnected bits helps us to see that life itself, lived out among the rest of us, is beautiful, complicated and mysterious.

Why don't we hear people's stories?

Part of the problem is perhaps that old age and infirmity can stretch over very many years. The earlier life gets lost in the battle against illness and we see the person just as they are near their life's end. But *once* they were not infirm. Once they were the people who felt they'd never get old or lonely or infirm. Can we get a grip on the life they lived and learn from it and see God's work in its patterns and weave?

Just before I was ordained a priest, my fellow ordinands and I had a visit from the then Bishop of London. I remember him commending to us the ministry of funerals and asking us to treat them with great reverence and tenderness.

He asked us not to spend too much time in our eulogy for the dead on their later years when they were sick. Instead, he asked us to celebrate their whole life and their younger selves too. 'Bring their stories to life,' he said. 'Celebrate them.' He wanted us to explore the life of the person more fully – partly to help us get away from the prevailing picture that old people are simply a pastoral issue. It was very good advice. I have attempted always to do this.

The Benedictine prayer[1] has it:

> God our Father
> open our eyes to see your hand at work
> in the splendour of creation,
> in the beauty of human life.
> Touched by your hand our world is holy.

Telling stories baptizes our everyday life with an inkling of God and claims for him a wider sphere of influence than we sometimes give him. It is also very encouraging to realize that it is really impossible to divide the stuff of life and the world around us from God interacting with it and us. If God is in all things, then we really begin to take stock.

> Telling stories baptizes our everyday life with an inkling of God.

I wonder how much I would be filled again with the awe of being alive if I took this to heart. In a world where so much seems to be wrong, becoming aware again that human life is beautiful and that the world, touched by God's hand, is holy, takes me to a different place – one of awe and wonder and gratitude.

Study questions

1. *As a parish priest, I became fed up with telling the amazing story of a person's life only when they died. At the end of a funeral people would come up and say they had no idea what an amazing life the person who died had. Why did we wait so long to find out?*

   What stories have you heard about people's lives at a funeral that have surprised you? What difference might it make if we knew more about the lives of those around us?

2. *The earlier life gets lost in the battle against illness and we see the person just as they are near their life's end. But once they were not infirm.*

   Discuss. What stories of the earlier life of people have you heard? Have any of them surprised you? What surprising facts about your own life might others be surprised to hear?

3. *Touched by your hand our world is holy.*

   How would we see the world if we saw it as holy and touched by God's hand? How would we see each other? What might it mean to say that the world has a kind of in-built holiness to it? Can you think of any examples?

Prayer

*Thank you for the people who have meant so much
to us. Help us to remember those who have been
before us and cherish all that they were.*

5

The Stories That Set Us Free

Whatever you have learned or received
or heard from me, or seen in me – put it
into practice. And the God of peace will
be with you.

Philippians 4:9

A paramilitary story

Jo Berry lost her father in the Brighton hotel bombing in 1984. Sir Anthony Berry was a Conservative MP. How can one deal with such a thing? Jo made contact with the IRA bomber Patrick Magee and a journey to reconciliation was begun. She now runs a charity called Building Bridges for Peace.

It was no easy journey for Jo and there were many painful twists and turns along the way. How must it feel to know that a stranger murdered your father?

At the heart of her journey and the road to reconciliation is the ability to listen to each other's story. As she put it at a conference in 2018 (Wounds that Heal, Harrow): 'The most powerful thing we have is that we care about them and will make room for their story as well.'

Jo heard Patrick and Patrick heard Jo. In doing so they 'rehumanised' each other. Patrick could no longer see Jo's dad as collateral damage – a political casualty. And Jo understood something of the real person that the demonized bomber was and is. It took a great deal of bravery to go through this process and also a level of trust. Perhaps more, it involved the acceptance of risk. There was no guarantee that there would be a happy ending.

God accepts risk is part of life. He risked everything in the mission of Jesus. It could have gone wrong at any moment. So, we too might also be prepared to take the risk of listening to a story that is uncomfortable and personal. Perhaps we cannot be truly free until we have worked on reconciliations of our own.

Jo and Patrick travel the world together now telling their story – the journey has not been easy. There have been bleak times and times when those around them have questioned what they are doing. Would it not be easier to stick to the old certainties and enmity?

A story told by a friend

I have always suffered with, as we used to call it, my nerves. We have lots of medicalized terms that we now use for this, but as long as I can remember I have had an up and down kind of life: sometimes I sail through life and at other times everything is an effort.

While I was studying theology at Oxford, I was going through a very bad time. I was beset by worries and troubling thoughts. I was clinging onto my faith by my fingertips and frequently thought about giving up. What kept me going was routine and burying myself in books. But the minute I thought about my life, a kind of deep and terrifying despair hit me all over again.

But if you were one of my course mates you'd never have known where I was really at. I have become an expert over the years in looking good, but feeling bad. As an aside, many, many people are good at presenting one face and feeling a completely different reality. This can be a very dangerous situation for them.

At this time, I had reached a low beyond most of the lows I had experienced and I was losing hope of ever being better.

One evening one of my course mates popped over to visit me. I liked him a lot. He was a gentle soul, quiet and shy. I am not sure what sparked it, but he told me something of his story and the troubles he was going through.

I listened, spellbound. His story was my story. He told me about his wrestling with his mental health over the years and it was so similar to my own travails that I began to feel better. I was not alone; there was hope.

We spoke into the early hours, and before my friend left for his own flat, we prayed together, and I confess that we both cried. It was such a relief. I had been expecting an evening of chatter; instead, I got something that had a lasting impact – and all from my modest, quiet and unassuming friend.

I admire my friend. I admire him because he was brave enough to tell me about himself and not the 'selfie' version of his life. It was a real risk to trust me with his story and I am happy that he felt I would listen and not judge. Through him I was able to tell my real story. I was able to be more honest.

I sometimes wonder whether, if aliens came to earth and discovered our phones, they would get a false picture of our lives. They would see happy families and smiling people. They would see excitement and travel and a life of leisure. But actually this is just a surface view. Most of us, perhaps, suffer angst and difficulties. We know the existential agony of life. Life is risky, it hurts.

Jesus lived a life like us and his experience included pain and tragedy. If we airbrush our life, we somehow dishonour the legacy of our God whose life was made up of light *and* shade. I felt oddly better that I could stop pretending about the difficulties I was facing.

That evening, because of the bravery of a person I was just beginning to get to know, I was able to get free from my wrestling with the problem of being human. It was the start of my long-term recovery.

Stories and health

One of the truths that many of us would ascribe to is that telling our stories is healthy – much healthier than keeping them to ourselves. Equally so, listening to another's story is a way to help them to heal and to help us to heal as well.

Historian Lucy Morrow puts it this way:

> Telling our stories is therapeutic. It is a primal human instinct to record and to tell. It is impossible to be human if we cannot tell our story or have no one to tell it to. We are a storytelling species and our stories perform a function . . . they codify our experience and make things clearer to us.[1]

Most modern people would probably buy into a therapeutic model of themselves and the world. We know that the health of our minds and emotions needs to be taken care of and that we can easily go wrong and become ill. In the absence of other cures, speaking the things that ail us is as good a tactic as any.

What we need is someone who is prepared to listen. But have we Christians lost the knack? Bonhoeffer[2] thought that we had. He argues that therapy and therapists have replaced the traditional role of the listening priest and church. He wonders if Christians have forgotten the great and holy ministry of listening. God, of course, is the great listener and we take our cue from him.

He is surely onto something. We have medicalized and professionalized the art and practice of listening to the stories of those in emotional distress. The act of active and attentive listening is sometimes the very best and most godly help we can offer anyone. But how often do we do it?

We are much more used to speaking openly about our struggles and our feelings. We accept that keeping things bottled up can be harmful and can make us ill. When we hear that the truth will set us free,[3] then we perhaps breathe a sigh of relief. No one wants to live a lie. No one wants to feel that they cannot be themselves – although that opens up so many questions about what 'our self' really is.

The truth sets us free

I wonder what it might feel like if we were to tell our story to the God who made the universe and everything in it. That would probably take quite a lot of courage, of course. My guess is that most of us would try to put a positive spin on it. We might be tempted to miss out some bits altogether. But there is an example in the Bible of a woman who wasn't afraid to be completely honest.[4] Indeed, she was open in a shocking way, perhaps.

Jesus is on one of his long walks – this time in Samaria – and he is tired and thirsty. It is good to see this human side of Jesus. He stops at a well and he starts a conversation with a local woman.

It is hot. Jesus breaks a taboo. Men, especially rabbis like Jesus, were not to talk to strange women, especially women on their own. But perhaps he is curious about this woman – especially why she is alone collecting water. He seems unruffled by the fact that she is also a Samaritan. For various theological reasons Jews and Samaritans didn't get on.

Jesus seemed to have a glorious curiosity about people's lives and was very prepared to be distracted and tarry a while and listen. Oh, how might we be more effective if we too were prepared to be distracted from all the important tasks we set ourselves. Jesus, of course, is even late for a death at one point – which was, to say the least, inconvenient for poor Lazarus (who was lying dead) and his desperate sisters.

It is roasting hot and an intriguing encounter follows.

A Samaritan woman comes to collect water. Now, she is an interesting character – she is bold and clever, but has a very mixed backstory. She has managed to run through a number of husbands and is now collecting water when none of the other more respectable women are around. I imagine that she was fed up with the knowing looks and comments. It was just easier to go and get the thing done when everyone else was avoiding the midday sun.

As mentioned above, there was a strict taboo on rabbis talking to women, especially women like this, but Jesus engages the unnamed woman in conversation.

What follows is a fascinating discussion – theological and personal. Jesus asks if she will give him a drink of water from the well. She, quite rightly, points out that Jews and Samaritans shouldn't be speaking. After some to-ing and fro-ing, Jesus makes an astounding offer of the water of eternal life.

The woman then makes a startling and brave admission. She shares a hidden part of her story that probably is covered with shame and denial. She could have kept things on a more impersonal level but she is awash, as it were, with hope. She wants a new start and the water of eternal life.

She confesses to Jesus that she has no husband and Jesus confirms that indeed she has had five husbands and is now living unmarried with another man.

There is nothing like this anywhere in ancient literature – indeed, it has a very modern feel.

The telling of her story sets the woman free. She is perhaps healed of guilt and feels able to start again. She begins to see herself differently. The events of her life are not as important as before.

We all live heavily edited and scrutinized lives. We might call them selfie-lives. If anyone hacked into our Facebook accounts then they might believe that we were the happiest citizens in the whole world. But of course, these are just the edited highlights and don't show the real us. Jesus knows much of the woman's backstory. He knows that she seems not to be one of the shiny, happy people who have got their life perfectly in order. It can be so hard when everyone else seems to have life worked out and running smoothly and our lives are an unmitigated mess. And what's more, everyone knows we are a mess.

But God among us seems completely unshocked by this woman's backstory. Indeed, he seems very comfortable to be near her. As Desmond Tutu said, 'We may be surprised at the people we find in heaven.

God has a soft spot for sinners. His standards are quite low.'

Would it be too much to say that he seems to enjoy her company and what she has to say?

As the conversation unfolds, Jesus does something incredible. Won over by this unnamed woman's honesty and desire for answers and for peace, he trusts her with a precious truth. He tells her that he is the Messiah. This is the first time he has done such a thing. It is a turning point. I wonder why he decided to tell this unnamed woman this secret. I don't think that he planned to. Perhaps he needed to get this 'fact' off his chest. After all, if he was just like us then he was allowed to feel the burden of his own story and destiny.

But that God would do such a thing is just about unthinkable. Think of the risk on Jesus' part. The woman could have laughed at him. She could have made fun. She could have ignored him.

The woman repays this by becoming the first evangelist. She goes back to her town and tells the story and encourages them to believe. She takes the truth that Jesus has offered and decides to share it. She does it not as a simple truth proposition though. No, she unfolds what has happened to those who listen as another story. She constructs a narrative that includes Jesus' revelation with her own story of encounter. She says, in John 4:29: 'Come, see a man who told me everything I've ever done.'

The telling of her story opened up something amazing. The freedom she felt, and the safe hands she was in, allowed her to say that God knows our story already, but he is still interested that we tell it.

We can echo the woman's call: 'Come, see a man who told me everything I've ever done.'

But the Samaritan woman goes deeper and tells the warts and all part of her life. That's what sets her free.

It's easy to miss Jesus' part in this. He helps her to get her story straight but he does not judge her.

The outcome is that she sees herself more clearly. Perhaps she no longer sees herself as a victim of circumstance. Perhaps she has a stronger sense of her identity. What we can say is that as a result of her encounter and her story exchange, she no longer feels defined by what has happened to her. The simple facts of her life are not what makes her, her. She is free.

She has engaged in a story that has healed her and an encounter that she will never forget.

'Bernal Heights'

There is a rather remarkable modern story of free-dom. Writer Hosanna Poetry has recorded, with musi-cal backing, a film of her striking spoken-word piece.[5] It adds a further dimension to the way stories heal.

The poet explains how much she hates the district of San Francisco called Bernal Heights. Her poem details why. It was the place where her father was a feared criminal who inflicted huge harm on her and the community. It is a place of dread for her and all she wants to do is to go away and never come back. It is too painful. Her father eventually contracted Hepatitis C and died, but not before coming to Jesus and being transformed. But even this transforma-tion cannot sweep away the emotional debris of the poet's early years.

To the poet, it looks as if the memories of all that happened might have poisoned the well of her hap-piness. But she takes a bold step and, drawing on Jesus' will for us to live life 'in all its fullness',[6] she decides to reclaim her story with the Lord at the centre of it.

As her act of making peace with her story she has her wedding in the very place where she suffered shame and pain as a child – Bernal Heights.

It is a powerful testimony of the way that ventilating our story leads to freedom. But that's only part of it. These days we have ways of commenting on stories and we can see how they impact.

> Ventilating our story leads to freedom.

There are simply hundreds of responses online to Hosanna Poetry's powerful life story. We see time and again the way it has spoken deeply to others – some in prison, some imprisoned by memories of their own fathers and birthplaces.

These testimonies show that stories – others' stories – have a way of influencing the way we see our own narrative. Telling our stories, it seems, might set others free as well.

Stories that do harm

People and churches tell themselves stories that can sometimes be harmful. Vaughan S. Roberts[7] describes this by saying that churches sometimes spread rumours about themselves. He describes a church that had taken to heart the story that it could not sing. This was inhibiting and damaging.

Roberts gets to the bottom of it by investigating the narrative. It turns out that a previous, very musical vicar had been harsh about the singing of the congregation and that the church had lost its ability to sing with confidence.

The only way was to tell a new story, and they did that by having fun with song again. They sang popular songs and the joy of raising their voiced returned.

Tucked away early in the Old Testament is the story of Ruth and her mother-in-law, Naomi. It is a story of the way we can predict disaster for ourselves without realizing that God has a say in such matters.

The story begins with the tragedy of a woman called Naomi who has lost her two sons. She is in the depths of despair. The two sons had two wives, and Naomi says that they should accept their freedom and go back to their homes and start again. One of the daughters-in-law accepts the offer and leaves. But Ruth is made of sterner stuff – she stays, although her prospects look bleak.

Naomi is in the middle of grief and hopelessness. She returns to her home town of Bethlehem. On her return the locals rally around her, but she is having none of it. In fact, she decides to rename herself to encapsulate her view of what her future story has to offer her.

'Don't call me Naomi,' she tells them. 'Call me Mara, because the Almighty has made my life very bitter.'[8]

She wants in future to be known by the name Bitter. It is rather like having a facial tattoo and shows the desperation of the woman. She simply feels that her story is at an end and that she is going to experience, and perhaps project, deep and abiding bitterness.

It is the kind of thing that Hosanna Poetry speaks about in her work, 'Bernal Heights'. She simply felt the prisoner of what had befallen her and could see no escape. She was defined by that story.

But for Naomi, as with the modern San Franciscan poet, the story was not over. There was a fresh turn of the page to come – thank God.

Ruth, Naomi's daughter-in-law, had not lost hope that there was a brighter future. And to be fair, Naomi was still full of practical wisdom, even if she felt that her own life was ruined. She does the right thing and offers some good advice to help Ruth find a new man.

The outcome is that Ruth marries an honourable and decent man called Boaz. Her life is turned around and she becomes part of the family line that eventually produces Jesus.

The book ends with 'bitter' Naomi, bitter no more. She is there with her grandson nestling in her lap, with her life renewed and her old age looking a better proposition than she had ever hoped for.

Ruth is one of the most beautiful books in the Bible. It has power because it has such psychological truth. At its heart is a message – don't call anything over till God calls it over.

Our stories are always only ever partly told; there is more to come and we need to be careful about proclaiming that where we are now is where we will stay.

A story without grace

But sometimes owning our story can be just too painful and difficult. Jephthah is from Gilead and becomes one of the major judges in that phase of Jewish history.

He has had an inauspicious beginning, which might explain his later actions. He is illegitimate. His mother was a prostitute. He is disowned by his family and has to flee.

He gathers around him a group of adventurers and becomes a mighty warrior – so much so that he is recruited by the elders of Gilead to fight their enemies.

Jephthah makes an unwise deal with God. He says that if he gains victory over the Ammonites, he will sacrifice whoever comes out of his family's house first when he returns.

He is victorious, but the first person through the door is his precious daughter. A couple of months later he kills her.[9]

It is a shocking story and we need to take care with it. Did God want the mighty warrior to sacrifice his daughter? Surely not. Perhaps it is a case of Jephthah making a fatal error. I have certainly read that the Jewish understanding of this story is that the killing is metaphorical, figurative. It is not that he killed her but that he no longer spoke to her (i.e. she was dead in his eyes).

He does not want to be humiliated in front of his men, instead he presses ahead and lives out the narrative that he cannot shed. Had he let in the grace and love of God, he might have told a new story altogether.

Perhaps he needed someone like Ruth around him to help him find a different ending.

Study questions

1. *Jo heard Patrick and Patrick heard Jo. In doing so they 'rehumanised' each other. Patrick could no longer see Jo's dad as collateral damage – a political casualty. And Jo understood something of the real person that the demonized bomber was and is. . . . Jo and Patrick travel the world together now telling their story – the journey has not been easy.*

   What do you think of this story? What are the rights and wrongs of it? Is it fair and should Jo have met her father's killer? What risks do we take when we listen to another's story? Would you take that risk?

2. *Jesus seemed to have a glorious curiosity about people's lives and was very prepared to be distracted and tarry a while and listen. Oh, how might we be more effective if we too were prepared to be distracted from all the important tasks we set ourselves.*

   Discuss. If we were happy to be distracted, how would it change our everyday lives? How much time do we give ourselves to be distracted?

3. *The Samaritan woman goes deeper and tells the warts and all part of her life. That's what sets her free.*

   Can you think of examples of stories setting either yourself or others free? How might this interaction have changed the Samaritan woman's life? What does it say about Jesus and his ministry, and what might we learn from it?

Prayer

*Help us take the risk of listening to the stories of
others with sensitivity and grace. As you listened
to the Samaritan woman, Lord, may we be bold
enough to offer our stories to you – to share our
lives as they really are. We don't want to pretend
to have airbrushed, perfect lives. Help us to be
aware of those who are putting on a cheerful front
but may be feeling desperate inside. If there are
colleagues or people close to us who are feeling
desperate and yet seem cheerful, please send your
Holy Spirit to counsel them and to encourage them
to get help.*

6

Jesus and Stories

Then you will call on me and come and
pray to me, and I will listen to you.

Jeremiah 29:12

Philip Yancey, in his show-stopping book *What's So Amazing About Grace*,[1] highlights the way that Jesus seemed to attract those who the world despised. Or, more particularly, he was trusted by those who the world despised. Jesus was a magnet for the dispossessed and the unglamorous. He specialized in extracting stories and being a very active listener, as we saw in the previous chapter.

Philip Yancey's book *What's So Amazing About Grace* is quite rightly a modern Christian classic. Yancey positions himself as the outsider and the critical friend of the church. He acknowledges that Jesus was, and is, a magnet for people who feel bad about themselves. We can share the whole story of our failure and hurt with him.

Like Bonhoeffer he wonders if the church has lost the knack of attracting the broken-hearted. Yancey can be very barbed about the church and wonders out loud if the church has lost the gist that Jesus had of being the only real place to be listened to and helped to feel better. He puts the point very abruptly – the down-and-out, the lost and lonely no longer feel welcome among the followers of Christ.

It is a sweeping statement but a good question. We need to ask ourselves if we *are* the place where people can come and trust us with their stories – especially when those stories are of personal disaster, mistakes and tragic decision-making.

I have been in churches that have seemed uncomfortable with such stories. They have been especially uncomfortable with the stories of those who are not healed from their addictions and afflictions. What to do with people – like us – who insist on continuing to fail, despite prayer ministry and the like?

But I have been in even more churches that listen with patience and understanding and do not fight shy of knowing that sometimes, despite everything, things go pear-shaped.

Now, we know that Jesus used stories as his primary method of communicating his message. He used intriguing and brief challenges called parables. The parables raise as many questions as they answer. There is much more to be said about these, but perhaps not here. What interests me is how Jesus listened and reacted to the life stories of the people he met. He had a way of drawing out revelations and tales that helped him and the person relating the stories to get to the centre of themselves.

> Stories have a way of lasting where polemic fails.

Part of Jesus' incarnational ministry is to be one of us and hear our stories and struggles – not as a voyeur but as God in the heart of life and honouring our lives. People did not present a CV to Jesus, but they did tell him something of their backstory.

Our insignificance is something many of us wrestle with – just look up on a clear night at the stars and see how much you feel yourself to be at the centre of the universe.

The woman

In chapter 5 of Mark's gospel, a woman comes out onto the streets to see Jesus. She has a good reason to be there. She is suffering with an unmentionable medical problem – so bad that in the purity code of the time it makes her both unclean and untouchable (an unpleasant combination). Indeed, she has spent just about all her money on doctors who have made the situation no better. One can only imagine what this meant and the procedures she underwent. She would have lost her money and probably suffered awful pain as well. Her hope must have drained to nothing and this was a last desperate act – what on earth was there to be done if this didn't work?

The woman is suffering from a gynaecological problem that results in her issuing blood. She hopes to
keep her story quiet and simply to touch Jesus' robes
and so be healed. In this way she can avoid shame.
The avoidance of shame is a common driving force.
She wants to keep her story to herself and hopes to
do business with God on a superficial level. In this
she stands in for many of us as we try to keep a po-
lite distance from the God who created the universe.

But it doesn't work out that way. She does indeed
touch Jesus' robes (and interrupts another healing
Jesus is engaged upon). The bleeding stops. You can
imagine her huge relief. The pain and shame are
over and no one got to find out. She can go home
and no one would be any the wiser. She can continue her life and not be changed in any way other
than the physical.

But in what must have been a moment of dread for
her, Jesus stops and asks the crowd who it was who
touched his robes.

I am sure that the woman must have toyed with
keeping quiet. But thankfully she doesn't. 'It was
me,' she says. And like Paul in his letter to the Galatians she reaches for autobiography. She does not
try to explain or justify herself other than trusting

Jesus with some of her life story. She does not say it was someone else, or someone else's fault.

With the story told, he gently says to her, 'Daughter, your faith has healed you. Go in peace and be freed from your suffering.'[2]

It is a heart-stoppingly tender moment. The loving God comforts her and calls her daughter. Oh, how she must have longed for this – the untouchable woman, the unclean person reclaimed as a daughter to be proud of and loved. One can imagine her heart flooded with gratitude and wonder. How could something so good happen?

And more than that, her faith has made her well. But what was the faith she showed? Yes, it was the faith that Jesus could heal her, but also the faith that he could be trusted with the full story. She believed that she could tell a man she had never met the thing that she did not want to reveal. She knew that her story had power and that perhaps her life wasn't a random series of happenings but instead a tapestry woven so that one day there would be a chapter on her meeting God in person.

Her story has been altered. We do not know what came next. We do not know what stories she told people about this day or how her life changed. We know just a small part of this precious woman's story – the woman without a name but with a biography.

The young man

For Jesus, the healings and the hubbub continue. He must have been exhausted. In a world with no effective medicine, there were always people who were desperate for healing. What's more, in a community that saw itself as God's chosen people there were so many questions to answer. That community was oppressed and under occupation. It was hard to know what made for a good life in such circumstances. There was a huge need for spiritual guidance and direction – just as there is now in our alienated world. People were desperate to know when God would make a reappearance and when their agony and humiliation would be over.

A young man comes literally sprinting up to see him. He has an urgent question that is troubling him. He has become anxious and worried about how he is to be saved. It is the kind of worry many of us have had. Perhaps there comes a time in every life when we ask this kind of question. It takes a few problems and trip-ups to wonder whether we can ever really be saved and safe. We wonder, as this man wonders, how we can lead the life that leads to God. How much of it can we do on our own – can we make ourselves good? The question rings down through the centuries – surely there is more to life than this?

The young man has an unusual problem (at least, it was unusual at a time when so many were poor and oppressed). He is rich. He asks Jesus what he has to do to get eternal life. He shares with Jesus the story of his striving for goodness his whole life. He explains that he is dedicated to trying to live out the Ten Commandments. Here is a man who has tried to do the right thing, and like many modern seekers he wonders whether this is enough.

Is it sufficient in life to try to be a nice person, to do no harm and to show vulnerable people across the road? Or is this a case of what sounds like a very modern self-delusion? Are we kidding ourselves if we think that just being quite nice is enough? If we look into our deepest hearts, is not what we see a huge vat of selfishness and self-regard? Are we no-where near as nice as we think we are and are we not helpless to really live the life we are called to without help from God?

Behind the personal autobiography are a range of hefty questions about what makes for the good life. They are the kinds of questions many of us have. The way we tell our life story is a revealing look at the big questions we have.

The young man trusts Jesus with this precious personal history. He has tried to be good. He has tried to be good by his own effort. It is a touching piece of self-disclosure. Many of us have tried and failed to be a better person. Many of us feel demoralized by this. But, I suppose, at least we have tried.

We are told that Jesus does two things – he looks at him and he loves him.[3] He loves him because he has been brave enough to share something of his story with the God who made the universe and now walks that very earth. He also sees something of the young man's seeking and his heart and desire for a life lived in fullness. God is open to the things we most desire.

The interaction turns out differently to the way the young man probably planned. Telling our stories can help us and others to see things more clearly and see what needs to change. Telling truthful stories is not risk-free. In the disclosure we make ourselves vulnerable and we sometimes expose areas where we simply have to make changes.

It is telling that Jesus' response is to look and to love. And would it be love if he left the story there? I think not. He takes the story and offers some poignant feedback.

Jesus says there is just the one thing that the young man now needs to do. Sell up all he has and give it to the poor, because his treasure will be in heaven. Then come and be my disciple, Jesus offers. It is an astounding offer.

One can imagine the silence as the young man thinks and weighs up his options. He perhaps for a moment wonders if he might just be able to do it. Perhaps he can give up his craving and need for money and possessions. Perhaps he could just stop his striving for things that don't make him happy and offer no real security – especially in an age with no banks or safe places to keep your wealth.

And then, we are told, his face falls and he goes away. Who knows if one day, as he gets older, he changes his mind? The little detail is poignant and beautifully drawn. He is sad, but he cannot give up his money. All is not lost, of course; he has the rest of his life to make the change that the Lord suggested.

The Bible has the ring of truth and the detail about the crestfallen young man is one of those moments. If it were a manifesto it would not have these small signifiers of reality and truth. It is, of course, moments like these that allow us to see the stories as true eyewitness accounts. They are true because they include the minor narrative details that signal that they were not just written to get a point across. The truth of the story is so striking that it bounces down through the centuries and we have it today as a gift. Stories have a way of lasting where polemic fails – and that is a great relief to us all.

The story of Jesus is full of interactions and in them people frequently trust him with some autobiography or insight into their deepest needs and wants.

When God was among us, he was distractible. He was prepared to stop and listen. I wonder how often we are prepared to do the same thing.

The incarnational God lived a life like us. He did things like us. He wasn't just an idea, he was alive. This points to an important fact. God was not like us in the abstract and does not love us in the abstract. This means that our lives are important to him.

The same story

I have a person in my congregation who has told me the same story about their life on dozens of occasions. That person has dementia. I try to treasure that story each time I hear it, as though I have not heard it before, because for them it seems like the first time they have told it to me. I will not become angry or annoyed at hearing it again – indeed I have begun to miss it when I don't hear it. I do not tell them off for telling me the story over and over again.

The story is about the time the person managed to get on the wrong bus and ended up in the wrong county. They then got on the wrong train and ended up even further from home. Finally, they made it back but had forgotten their key.

I have grown to love the consistency of the story and the way it makes the teller smile each time. I love the way they anticipate me being surprised and delighted. I like the picture of the lovely sunny day that it happened on and the fact they were wearing their poshest clothes for the day out. The current day is misted-up and a mess, but this day still shines as brightly as ever. And all it needs is there to be someone available to listen to that story and to find delight in it.

As people begin to lose their memories they are left with stories. They are one of the last things to go. We feel that the people we knew are slipping away, but they can often still tell us a story and we can listen to it. Those stories capture old times or times when life was less perilous. They say something about our deep need to keep certain things alive and to value our lives and experiences.

The story is a gift. It is precious even though I have heard it before. It is a gift because in the chaos of this person's dementia it offers the hope that life does make sense and that our stories add up to a life that has value.

In chapter 17 you will hear what happened when, as a church, we encouraged a group of people who had known each other at church for years to tell their life stories.

Study questions

1. *The down-and-out, the lost and lonely no longer feel welcome among the followers of Christ.*

   Do you agree with Yancey's view? In what ways might this be true or untrue? Are there ways we could be more open to stories?

2. *Part of Jesus' incarnational ministry is to be one of us and hear our stories and struggles.*

   Why does he listen to people and how does this affect them? What might it say about the nature of God and his time among us? What can we learn from this?

3. *When God was among us, he was distractible. He was prepared to stop and listen. I wonder how often we are prepared to do the same thing.*

   Discuss. How busy are we? How able are we to take time away from that busyness?

Prayer

*Father, we want to learn from the stories of the sick
woman and the young man. Would you help us to
do this? Help us to see the road to freedom and the
way we can deal with things that are troubling us.
Put people in our paths who can tell us a story and
we can travel beside. Let us never give up believing
that things are not beyond your transformation,
even those we have prayed about for many years.*

PART TWO

Telling Stories

7

Jesus the Storyteller

Jesus answered, 'It is written: "Man shall not live on bread alone, but on every word that comes from the mouth of God."'

Matthew 4:4

We know how much Jesus valued the stories of the precious people who flocked to him. But he was also a master storyteller.

When asked to explain an important theological point – for instance, 'who is my neighbour?'[1] – he resists the temptation to simply give a list of facts. Instead, he answers with a story . . . a 'Once upon a time'.

The story has a location and a timeframe and a protagonist and an antagonist – just like all classic stories. In this case, it involves a foolish traveller who gets himself mugged and left for dead. The cast includes pious religious folk who pass by on the other side, an innkeeper, and a good Samaritan who acts against type.

The end result of this narrative is that we can be in no doubt about who our neighbours are. But perhaps most interestingly, we have the kind of story that has had traction.

The story of the Good Samaritan has passed into cultural reference and is known around the world. It is a story that doesn't really involve stock characters. It is told with glorious authorial

> The story of the Good Samaritan has passed into cultural reference.

precision with characters drawn with fine brush strokes. It involves the kind of dilemma that we all face – when to do good if it is inconvenient for us.

It also involves peril, stupidity and altruism. Because of this it is deeply memorable and makes the point about the value of narrative. When we hear stories, the dilemmas people face come alive, and we can sometimes see how God was working in these.

I was walking past Parliament at the time of the Brexit furore. Standing by a newscaster was a shaven-headed man with a poster. For some reason the sheer futility of this annoyed me. I stopped and we spoke. He explained to me that he had spent the last of this week's pension to come down from Manchester to bring his poster and be on his lonely vigil. He told me he was doing this, not for himself, but for his grandchildren.

My unreasonable annoyance vanished. I saw before me a parent, just like me, and a man who was determined to try to make a difference. His story opened me up to empathy. But there was more to follow. I told him that I was a priest. He was exceptionally positive. Then he asked: 'What does God think of Brexit?'

It was a good question. I explained that I didn't know, but that I was sure God was on the side of free speech and debate, and fairness and justice.

My new friend and I shook hands and he wished me a cheery, 'Happy Christmas, Father.'

Study questions

1. *When asked to explain an important theological point – for instance, 'who is my neighbour?' – he resists the temptation to simply give a list of facts. Instead, he answers with a story . . . a 'Once upon a time'.*

   Why does he do this? How might this tactic help us as we meet and interact with others?

2. *My unreasonable annoyance vanished. I saw before me a parent, just like me, and a man who was determined to try to make a difference. His story opened me up to empathy.*

   How does empathy change the way we see people? Can you think of some examples of your own?

Prayer

I am so often tempted to pass by on the other side. I want to avoid the pain of others and not get involved in their messiness. I settle for stock responses and easy stereotypes. I do not see the person behind the mask and retreat into my own comfort zone. Bring people to me to help me break away from my complacency and pride. Forgive me, Lord, for I have sinned.

8

What Storytellers Teach Us

I had always felt life first as a story: and
if there is a story there is a story-teller.

G.K. Chesterton, *Orthodoxy*

As well as being a storytelling species, we are an art-making species. As far as we can tell, no other creature makes or needs art as we do. My cats are perfectly happy to spend the whole day sleeping, eating and catching mice – in that order.

Pádraig Ó Tuama in his beautiful book, *In the Shelter*[1] speaks of the time he nearly said goodbye to God. His faith was at an all-time low and so was he. Partly he had questions about his sexuality and who he was. His faith background had left him battered. He felt like giving up, but decided to have one more shot at rekindling his faith, but what kind of faith?

He decides to go to a monastery – a kind of attempt at an extended farewell to God. He takes with him some books – theology and fiction and poetry. Each perform a different function. The fiction holds his attention. The poetry burrows deep into his soul. And with the influence of both of these he begins to see the theology differently.

Exposure to the trinity of poetry, fiction and theology begins to change his view of what faith really is. He had gone into this final roll of the dice despairing, because his past had told him that faith was about certainty; now he began to think again. What if faith allowed for doubt?

Rather than say goodbye to God he starts a different kind of path with him. The books and poetry and culture allow him to be less rigid and somehow more positive. The books perform the task that great books always seem to – they open up the reader to new possibilities and horizons – even if one of these horizons is an increase in healthy doubt. They allow Ó Tuama to seriously and properly become a pilgrim open to a wider palette of emotions and influences.

Stories and art are more than a pastime. Sometimes they seem like all that we have.

We cannot go far when thinking about the stories we tell without bumping into art, and especially the novelist's craft. Perhaps the thirst for fiction might tell us something about the importance of stories. Perhaps, also, we can see something of the novelist's craft in the stories we all tell.

The power of fiction is a mystery in some ways. Why should made-up stories have such an impact on us? Why should we crave them and why do they seem so much more than simple entertainment? There's a long-standing argument that fiction, and especially serious fiction, is good for us because it causes us to be more empathetic. We get to experience

> Why should made-up stories have such an impact on us?

things and people and situations that we wouldn't otherwise do. But is this enough to explain the effect of stories? I don't think so.

Perhaps if we look at our love of fiction, we might get an insight into why our own personally constructed life-tales are quite so important to us.

Frederick Buechner[2] in his masterful collection *Secrets in the Dark* makes an explicit connection between faith and fiction. For him, the two are so alike that we need to take heed.

With faith, he explains, we begin to make connections between the God who is close and in our own lives. We see patterns – or at least we hope that we see patterns. Faith isn't a set of truth propositions; it is the weaving of our story with the great story of salvation and creation.

In fiction and in faith what really matters are the people you meet, the things that happen and the places you end up in. Buechner points out that in both faith and fiction we start from 'Once upon a time'. Both fiction and faith are part of growth and change.

In both faith and fiction, we need to pay attention to what's happening. If we start skipping pages then we lose our love of books. We need to pay attention to the details of our lives and the stories of those around us, for in them we get a sustaining hand on our faith and insight into the mystery and beauty of God, of human life and the life of the creation around us.

In fiction, events follow events. Time unfolds. People come and go and, in the end, time runs out. When you think of it, our life and our faith have much in common with this narrative line.

The novelists and the novel

The novel as we know it is a relatively recent invention. The kind of novels that we read now began in the eighteenth century in England and largely as the result of an emerging middle class who had time on their hands and journeys to work to fill. Early novels were often written in weekly instalments – which probably explains all the cliffhangers. They were designed to both keep people reading and to entertain and to amuse and, yes, sometimes to educate.

The novel took off because it told stories that resonated with people's lives at the time. People wanted an art form that was theirs – and the novel has always been *our* art form.

I have long thought that if Jesus had not come 2,000 years ago and instead was with us now, our response would not be to write a history about him, but to construct a novel. Although, of course, the gospel stories do have much in common with the novel – they have twists and turns, cliffhangers, people who come and go and a narrative timeline.

Good stories make us better people

My teachers were old-school. They believed that good books help to make us more civilized, more empathetic and open up something deep within our souls. Good books are good for us. Despite going through two university degrees at the time when postmodernism and semiotics were all the rage and literature was stripped of moral authority and the power to improve, I still go along with my old teachers.

I am a transformed person because I met up with Jesus Christ, but books have made me a more understanding and wiser person too.

So, what can we learn from literature and the wealth of its stories told? Can an appreciation of fiction help us understand how to do storytelling better in our

Christian communities? Can the power of fiction help us to understand not just the big story of God but the telling of our own little histories?

Stories need listeners, but they also need people bold enough to tell their own story and to know that they have value. Art is a living commitment to storytelling.

C.S. Lewis spoke about that 'deeper magic' – the sense of the marvellous and strangeness of life that cannot be rationalized away and can't be described in a science book. There is a kind of ancient magic at the heart of life. It takes stories to remind ourselves of how marvellous our world is and how odd it sometimes seems.

Frank Kermode's masterful book *The Sense of an Ending*[3] has something interesting to say about just why stories are so important. His thesis is that we all search for significance in our random and uncertain existence. Most of us have a sense that we are here for but a short time and that one day the world will end apocalyptically. Others struggle with a sense of their own meaninglessness – that their lives are simply a set of random events.

But novels place a sense of beginning, middle and end on proceedings. Plots tidy up loose ends and this can bring a sense of how we are more than a set of loose ends as well. Fiction gives us a sense of order. We humans need this.

Again, there is something in this. Art is a way of processing life and helping us to see it afresh. It is surely not really a set of signs and symbols and every book is not simply a reworking of other books – a kind of extended exercise in literature quotation and admiration. Novels, stories, perform a valuable task – they give us a sense of an ending and without this kind of sense we can descend into randomness and chaos.

Fiction teaches us that stories are part of being a person. And, if truth be told, we all fictionalize our own life stories just a little. That doesn't matter, it is part of the great creativity of humans, and our embellishments are just a way of adding a bit of flavour to our lives.

The naked civil servant

Quentin Crisp, the great doyen of New York alternative culture and 'naked civil servant', made an art form of his own life story. Crisp was a fixture on the New York art and cultural stage. He was a commentator on the times.

Crisp's life story became a strange work of art. (Lady Gaga might be his modern-day equivalent.) What he had was the life that he had lived in the period through which he had lived and the places in which it had happened. His story spoke hope into many others' lives and he enjoyed telling it. Just before his death he received a speaking engagement in England – to come and tell his story one more time.

He knew that he was unwell and those who loved him urged him to stay safe at home in NYC. (They didn't think he would survive the journey.) But he decided to come back to the motherland. He had a job to do – the job that he had dedicated his life to. He had a story to tell – of overcoming prejudice, of self-expression and a love of art and language. What was he if not the architect of the telling of a life story? And his life story was the most precious gift he had – even when ill and infirm.

That was his last trip. He died back in England on the day before his show opened – surely there was something fitting in that. He left very little money in his will. His flat in NYC was piled high with junk and the debris of his chaotic life. But where few of his contemporaries are remembered – the life lived of this slight and fragile dandy is still treasured.

But if we take Crisp seriously for a moment, he hints that our own stories are just like art – they have the same status and worth as a good novel. They have that same sense of reality and the same ability to teach lessons and paint pictures that allow us to understand ourselves a little more. Thus, we begin to see how our stories can be transformative. They have the same flavour and function. Crisp's example seems to say to us that we each have one great story to tell – that of our own lives.

We may not have *the* great novel in us, but we do have the novel of our own life.

We must be storytellers . . . or else

Charles Causley, that great old post-war poet, said that stories must be got 'out'.[4] He argued that being a poet or a storyteller was more than a hobby. If we left a story untold it could do untold damage to our souls, our health.

The need to tell stories is a powerful urge. It was one that the Gospel writers understood.

Dickens too was a compulsive storyteller, although in his case, fiction. I believe he lived for telling stories;

it is what drove him on. (Scholars of Dickens though will tell you that much of his output mined and used the dark soil of his childhood.) His fiction had more than a hint of faction about it.

Dickens was ill, fraught and getting older. He was invited to go to the States for a storytelling tour. He had a punishing schedule and, by the end, could not eat solid food. He lived on champagne and eggs beaten into sherry. Back at home in the UK he was ill, and not that long after, he died, having suffered a stroke.

Everywhere he went, Dickens did readings because people loved his work. He wanted to see people hearing his stories. He wanted to weave that old magic which is creating an imagined world.

Our appetite for novels points to an even greater need for stories that matter and perhaps the greatest need – to know that our stories matter.

Also, of course, stories can sometimes make points that simple propositional truth is powerless to make. Take the case of the show at the Edinburgh Fringe.

Stories get to the heart of the matter

As a Christian minister, the Fringe asked so many questions of me. How do I get my information? How do I learn from the amazing artistic endeavours and communication skills in this, the greatest arts festival in the world? How might we make church as challenging, thoughtful and inclusive as the arts seem to manage to do?

The most beautiful show I saw was called *Paradise Lodge.* It was so wonderful that I have booked the company to come to St Cuthbert's, North Wembley to perform it.

The play is set in a care home for people with dementia. It features an old-style duo performing wartime songs to a mainly comatose audience. But along the way it deals with the themes of tragedy and hope and memory. It also tackles the horrible feelings of hopelessness that we all feel when faced with the enormity of the difficulties associated with failing health. Why spend time with people in care homes when they seem to no longer know who you are or who they are themselves?

I have been running a memory café for four years and have written countless articles on it. These are good and worthy pieces of writing.

But this one-hour drama got to the heart of loving people with dementia. Art opened up the heart of the issue and helped us to see things from different perspectives. It worked because it wasn't didactic.

It didn't tell us what to believe. It was not about doctrine or propositional truth. Instead it gently unfolded a story about life, and it let that story and those other lives speak into our hearts.

It managed to help us to see the issue afresh, but more importantly to feel afresh. At the end of it, I felt again that what we are doing at memory café is of huge significance. Any work anyone does to ease the pain of others is God's work.

I am already looking forward to going back to the Fringe next year. But I do not want to lose what the festival gave me this year. I want to carry it and pass it on to others.

The festival is remorseless. Show follows show and it is tempting to think that what happens here is ephemeral. But as I cried quietly in the back row of *Paradise Lodge*, I renewed my commitment to never give up helping others and remembering that 'the last will be first'.[5]

Mark's inspiring story

Mark's story is sketched in the New Testament although we have to dig a little to find it. His personal story speaks to us as much as the story he wrote down about Jesus. Mark's ups and downs are an encouragement to those of us who have suffered the odd defeat in life and not been tough enough when needed.

We gather that Mark may have had a dark night of the soul and a defeat that looked like it might be the end of him, and his useful ministry. He was well-connected and probably had lived a life of ease and comfort. He was possibly a bit pampered and perhaps was a sensitive soul.

In a fit of zeal, he signed up to accompany Paul and his uncle Barnabas on one of Paul's missions. These missions were not for the faint-hearted. They involved much privation, great danger and suffering. It would have helped to have an army training to get through them. We miss how unforgiving the terrain was and how primitive the surroundings. Danger was everywhere and not just from the humans – but from wild animals and the forces of nature. It was no easy business travelling in the ancient world – especially if you did it without an armed escort.

We are not sure why, but at some point in the mission he decided he couldn't go on and that he wanted to come home. Perhaps life on the road was too tough. My hunch is that he was homesick and couldn't face the next stage of the journey which probably involved climbing steep hills and difficult terrain.

Paul appears to have been dismissive and perhaps furious. He wants to cut the boy off. He feels let down and one can almost hear his contempt for the young man, Mark.[6] But kindly Barnabas accompanies Mark home and rebuilds his confidence. He can see something in the young man. He is not prepared to give up on him yet. In fact, this is a major split because Barnabas and Paul themselves seem to fall out over what happens.

For Mark this whole episode must have been humiliating. Rather than returning home as the bold faith warrior, he came home as the boy who couldn't stand the pressure. No man likes to look weak. I am sure that Mark's relatives did their best to comfort him, but he must have blushed with shame and perhaps felt he would never be strong enough, or good enough.

Years later, the same Mark gets to become a hero of the faith and writes one of the Gospels. Indeed, even Paul acknowledges how useful he has become.[7] In fact, Paul needs to see Mark again because he is feeling anxious and alone.

He is rehabilitated. Mark may not have been a tough missionary, at least not as a young man, but his pen spoke mightier than any of his other actions. His great talent was writing down a story that went on to change the world.

This personal story has the strong ring of truth about it. It is easily missed and has to be unpicked from fleeting mentions in Paul's letters. We can only imagine how important Mark's personal story was in his amazing story as a follower of Jesus. In the end, he knew that his life could be forfeit, but the story he wrote down and the inspiring story of his life would live on forever. And in some sense, that's true of all of us.

And there's one more thing about Mark. His gospel ends mid-sentence. Why was that? Of course, the rest could just have been lost or mislaid. But it seems more likely to me that he ends it mid-sentence because Mark was interrupted – possibly from his prison cell as he was taken out to be martyred.

Mark has to write the story. It is perhaps the last thing he has to do. So urgent is the need for this story that he keeps going almost until his last breath. Telling stories isn't a confection for Mark. Storytelling has a compulsion about it and urgency.

It is his life's great work and I wonder if he felt anxious that he had not managed to get to the final full stop. One day we will find out.

Study questions

1. *He decides to go to a monastery – a kind of attempt at an extended farewell to God. He takes with him some books – theology and fiction and poetry.*

   How have theology, fiction and poetry changed your relationship with God? What might they add to your life and why are they so important?

2. *Novels, stories, perform a valuable task – they give us a sense of an ending and without this kind of sense we can descend into randomness and chaos.*

   Discuss. What is the role of fiction? How does it help us to see life anew?

3. *Mark's ups and downs are an encouragement to those of us who have suffered the odd defeat in life and not been tough enough when needed.*

   In what ways are Mark's story inspiring? What other New Testament characters inspire you and why?

Prayer

Thank you for all the creative things we do and for the artists, poets and novelists of this world. Thank you that we can read and for all the joy art brings. Thank you for the way our lives are transformed by creativity. You are the heart of all that is creative and we thank you for that. Encourage our creativity and help us to be encouragers of creativity in others.

9

Paul Tells His Story – And Ditches the Theology

> Jesus did not let him, but said, 'Go home to your own people and tell them how much the Lord has done for you, and how he has had mercy on you.'

Mark 5:19

What about the other architect of the faith – Paul? Here was a man who knew his scripture and was a stickler for detail. Was there poetry in his soul and an ear for a story?

Perhaps surprisingly, the answer was a resounding yes.

Paul was a troubled genius. He worried, and on one occasion he is worrying about one of his tender young churches. Not to put too fine a point on it, it seems to be going to pot. More particularly, it is having problems sticking to the truth of the faith – it is being blown off course by false teachers.

You'd probably imagine that a clever man like Paul would counteract this problem with a good dose of teaching, with some solid theology perhaps.

Orthodoxy is at stake and Paul is probably worrying that the church might collapse. We sometimes forget what a tender plant the early church was. It would not have taken much for it to fail. Paul was all too aware of how his infant churches needed to be nurtured and managed. But how was he to do it – what weapons did he have?

Paul doesn't have a lot of options at his command. He begins by deciding to dictate and send a letter. He can't get there in person and there are none of the wonders of the technology we have at our disposal. Writing is his option, and for a man who may have suffered from a debilitating eye condition, writing would have been difficult. But there is an imperative – he has to get a message through. But what kind of message?

Paul crafts a letter for the Galatian church. He is anxious to establish his credentials – something that surfaces again and again in his ministry. It is more than probable that he was often called-out as a fraud and not a proper follower.

Paul was not an eyewitness, as the other apostles were. He had also been a persecutor of the early church. And so, he begins with his calling card:

> Paul, an apostle – sent not from men nor by a man, but by Jesus Christ and God the Father, who raised him from the dead – and all the brothers and sisters with me . . .
>
> Galatians 1:1–2

Paul needs to establish on whose authority he speaks and to reassure his readers, and perhaps himself, that he is the real deal. He reminds his readers of the royal commission he has received.

Interestingly, he mentions the many helpers who cluster round him and sustain him. Paul was a man who liked to have companions. I often think he got especially miserable when he was on his own – with only his lonely thoughts for company. And in this letter, we get a glimpse of the band of people who accompanied him and built him up. Even the great Paul needed support and help. Perhaps he took comfort from their tales and the stories of how the faith was prospering.

The letter is astounding. It is astounding for a particular reason: because, rather than solve his problem with theology, he decides to begin somewhere completely different. He begins with autobiography. He reaches for a personal story, because a story is the most powerful weapon he has.

Paul has a profound insight – his life tells a story and that story has power if people are prepared to listen. Simple propositions of truth have always been of limited value unless they are backed up with something else – experience.

> Paul has a profound insight – his life tells a story and that story has power.

Paul's story as a gift

Paul reminds his readers of the story of old, of how he had been a persecutor of Christians. How he had tried to destroy the church and how he *was* a high-flier, a swiftly rising star, in the party of the Pharisees. He explains that after his conversion he simply took time out to process what had happened. He wasn't one of the in-crowd, the inner circle of the apostles. He was probably always held in suspicion.

He explains that after three lonely years he eventually went to Jerusalem and there spent time with Peter, although that only amounted to fifteen days. It must have affirmed Paul, although perhaps he wondered why he didn't get to see the rest of the inner circle. The Jerusalem church still held Paul at arm's length.

Perhaps he was still toxic and a bit too hot to handle. But at least he was in from his own Siberia – he met with one of the leaders of the Jerusalem church – and that must have been some affirmation.

The story goes on, and you can read it in Galatians 1:11–21. It is easy to miss its significance. Paul has to tell his life story and to let it speak for him. He has to tell it not just for the Galatians, but for himself. His story is what he has, and he is at least fortunate to have people to tell it to.

It is a tragic fact that many, many people in our at-omized world have no one who wants to hear their story. Many older people, for example, do not see a living soul all week. Many wonder if their life story has value, and as they wonder that, their life itself seems to be a devalued currency.

When Paul's faith is low and people doubt him – as they often do – he takes time to tell the old story of his life. Paul was a man who saw himself as 'the worst'[1] of all sinners, so he had esteem problems. In modern parlance, we would probably diagnose the great saint as suffering from depression and anxiety. Some may baulk at this, but his letters suggest this diagnosis so completely that it is hard to dodge. Paul suffered both physically and mentally, and yet he was made of stern stuff – most notably his unshakeable faith in Jesus.

When he heard the internal whispers, and perhaps doubt came crowding in, he reached for the story he knew best. He retold it to give himself hope and to frame the faith for the sapling church he had planted.

Our need for stories

Perhaps we all need to tell our story. 'Once upon a time' is a phrase of the utmost power. It is one that most of us have heard from our earliest days as our parents or guardians told us stories.

We need to take our time with our stories; we need to say them in front of others, and that can make us feel vulnerable and takes courage. There is nothing so guaranteed to make a person feel as if they don't exist than to have no one to listen to their story.

But why did Paul, the great evangelist, feel the need to tell a story about himself? Yes, it was a barrier to his own insecurity. Yes, it bolstered his credentials and he was perhaps fed up with having to keep justifying himself. But I think Paul is onto something even more important.

Paul, like us, was not an actual eyewitness to the Jesus who walked the earth, although he did have an encounter. He was a convert and as such has more in common with us than any other person in the Bible. If he wasn't a witness, he couldn't tell directly the stories of Jesus' healings and the like; he never saw them.

As Paul was not an eyewitness, he realized he had a different kind of story. He had to be a different kind of witness . . . he had his own story to tell, that was what he had to vouch for. It is what we have to vouch for too. The other followers, like John and Peter, don't seem to have had such a pressing need to tell their story, although we do hear some of it. The real imperative for them was that they were there – they saw it all.

Study questions

1. *Rather than solve his problem with theology, he decides to begin somewhere completely different. He begins with autobiography. He reaches for a personal story, because a story is the most powerful weapon he has.*

   Why does Paul do this? What was his thinking? How might your story carry weight with others? When might be a good time to tell it and can you recall times when experiencing the autobiography of another person helped you to think again?

2. *When he heard the internal whispers, and perhaps doubt came crowding in, he reached for the story he knew best. He retold it to give himself hope and to frame the faith for the sapling church he had planted.*

   Discuss. How might Paul's story have encouraged the church and encouraged him? Are there times when you go back to the story of why you have a faith? How does this encourage you? In what way does autobiography help you to deal with doubt?

3. *Perhaps we all need to tell our story. 'Once upon a time' is a phrase of the utmost power. It is one that most of us have heard from our earliest days as our parents or guardians told us stories.*

How do you respond to this thought-provoking suggestion? Explore why 'Once upon a time' is so powerful. Do the Gospels plug into this deep need for creating a story to explain reality?

Prayer

*Father, we all sometimes need the security of 'Once
upon a time'. We need to frame our experience
and our lives in terms of a story with a beginning,
middle and end. Sometimes our story rekindles our
hope and reminds us of who we are and whose
we are – just like Paul experienced. Thank you that
our stories have value and that we are more than
just a set of random happenings and experiences.
When we feel insecure and in peril, remind us of the
strength of our life story and bring to mind, too, the
encouraging life stories we have heard from others.
When people doubt us and we feel demeaned,
bring us strength and comfort in your abiding love.
Thank you for the love that won't let go and your
promise to always be with us.*

10

Telling Stories in Emergency Situations

Christendom has had a series of
revolutions and in each one of them
Christianity has died. Christianity has died
many times and risen again; for it had a
God who knew the way out of the grave.

G.K. Chesterton, *The Everlasting Man*

It took a clown to bring out a story

Roly Bain was an Anglican priest and a clown. He proudly claimed to have thrown custard pies into the faces of ten bishops and that they didn't mind – much. He helped set up Holy Fools, a loose-knit confederation of people committed to clowning in worship and ministry.

In his book *Playing the Fool*, he tells a heart-warming tale of the power of stories. While performing at a hospice, he was made aware that one of the regulars in the audience had died.

The rest of the audience and Roly were moved into another room as the orderlies put up protective screens around the deceased. None of us are comfortable with the actuality of death.

Roly the Holy Clown broke the awkward silence and told a touching fable to those who were there – a story of a dying clown who made a statue of a sad infant Jesus laugh. The listeners had just confronted their own mortality in the starkest way. Just behind a hospital screen was the fate that awaited them all – indeed, awaits *us* all.

The power of the story was palpable. It dealt with death and life and joy and the ability of the humble fool to make even the Creator of the universe see things in a different light. At the end of the clown's tale the mood had changed. Roly explains that it allowed people to start to come to terms with the idea and actuality of terminal illness and death.[1]

Bain reflects that stories provoke more stories and those stories can set us free.

As we read the Bible, we see examples of this deep truth planted there. We see people speaking about their lives and this having a transforming effect on them.

Jesus on the lonely road with his friends

Towards the end of Luke's Gospel (24:13–34) he recounts a strange story of a meeting on a lonely road. Two of Jesus' followers are heading home after the death of Jesus. One is called Cleopas, the other is unnamed.

The two are downcast. It seems to them that the dream is over – all that they had hoped of from Jesus' ministry had come to nothing. Perhaps we have all had moments like this. We know what it is like to feel ourselves at the end of something that we had passionately hoped for.

> We see people speaking about their lives and this having a transforming effect on them.

It was a dangerous road indeed, plagued by robbers and dark and difficult. No sane person would be out on it even with a companion – certainly not alone.

The two dejected followers are joined by a man who engages them in conversation. He asks them what they are talking about and their incredulous response speaks much about the waves the death of Jesus caused. They comment that he must be the only person in or travelling from Jerusalem who hasn't heard about the execution of Jesus. Intriguingly they have heard the testimony of the women who have seen the empty tomb and declared the resurrection but they don't believe it.

After another exchange, they invite the stranger to come and stay with them. After all, it is very dangerous on that road and the night is drawing in.

It is then that a magnificent event happens. As the two companions and Jesus sit down to eat, they realize who he is.

So transformed are they that they go back immediately to Jerusalem, risking the perilous road to tell the followers that Jesus is risen.

I often wonder about the meeting on the road and what they talked of. I am more than hopeful that they exchanged stories as well as spending time deep in the Scriptures – otherwise it might have seemed a very long journey indeed.

The Gospels only give us a partial picture. We hear about Jesus' healings and some of his scrapes and his enigmatic teaching. Rabbis used to teach by asking questions and positing wild juxtapositions to help people to break free from rigid thinking. But what we don't have are the ordinary stories that Jesus surely exchanged with the people he met.

I find it hard to believe that his followers would have stuck with him without the glue of shared stories and small-talk. I would love to know if Jesus shared the kind of stories that this book is about. About the time he went with his father to work, or the time his brother made him laugh or the time his family meal went all wrong and his mother had to start it again.

We don't hear about him and his followers having a great laugh about some of the ups and downs of being travelling teachers and evangelists. G.K. Chesterton in his book *Orthodoxy*,[2] laments that despite the Christ being drawn in bold primary colours and being a colossus, we do not get an insight into his mirth. Chesterton argues that he hid this from us and perhaps kept it for his quiet times with his Father.

If I could time travel, I would love to go and sit with Jesus and the disciples and hear their stories. I feel sure that it was stories as well as the teachings and miracles that held them together and helped them to understand each other.

One of the reasons I am sure that there were stories is that there seems to be a human impulse to tell them. Or more particularly, a deep need to tell our own story (and sometimes our fictional ones) to others.

Jesus leaves behind stories; others do as well.

Study questions

1. *I often wonder about the meeting on the road and what they talked of. I am more than hopeful that they exchanged stories as well as spending time deep in the Scriptures.*

   Discuss. How might the conversation have gone? How might this conversation have inspired the listeners over the years that followed?

2. *I find it hard to believe that his followers would have stuck with him without the glue of shared stories and small-talk. I would love to know if Jesus shared the kind of stories that this book is about. About the time he went with his father to work, or the time his brother made him laugh or the time his family meal went all wrong and his mother had to start it again.*

   If we begin to imagine this picture, how do we see Jesus afresh? Does he seem more human and real? What might it have been like being on the road with Jesus day-to-day?

3. *If I could time travel, I would love to go and sit with Jesus and the disciples and hear their stories. I feel sure that it was stories as well as the teachings and miracles that held them together and helped them to understand each other.*

How do you respond to this? What might life have been like and how would sharing these everyday events and stories have shaped Jesus' view of the world and his ministry? How might such easy and happy fellowship transform our own faith journeys and church itself?

Prayer

Father, please help us to know it is more than OK to have a laugh with our friends and share silly stories and jokes. Help us and our churches to be light of heart and to enjoy just being alive and taking pleasure in all that surrounds us. Let us learn from that meeting that Jesus had with his discouraged followers.

If we feel discouraged, let us gather and tell stories, eat together, drink a pint of ale and sing songs of happiness and gratitude. Help us to take ourselves less seriously and you more seriously.

11

Who Gets to Tell Their Story?

No one heals himself by wounding another.

St Ambrose

A lesson for Christians

Chris Armstrong in his book *Medieval Wisdom for Modern Christians*[1] has a spiky critique of us modern folk. He says that we are infected with the need to have everything immediately.

It is fair to say that he reserves his most persistent criticisms for the modern evangelical church. He argues that we are obsessed with simple, quick unmediated prayers with God and quick fixes. Our focus is upwards and not outwards. We forget to also connect with those we share our lives and communities with.

Without twisting Armstrong's insights too much, that horizontal relatedness must surely include listening to those around us and building up real family ties with them.

Perhaps the issue is that we need to cast our net a bit wider to hear those who have not been heard. There is a world of people whose stories have been suppressed.

> There is a world of people whose stories have been suppressed.

The lost and the unglamorous and the oppressed still struggle to be heard. Partly this is surely due to the fear that these stories might force us to make changes to the way that we live. If we open up to these stories, we may need to examine our own hearts and conduct.

So, who gets to tell the best stories? Who should we actually be listening to?

The Beatitudes[2] begin to give us a clue. Blessed are the poor and the meek and the bereaved. Oddly, these are three groups who we rarely get to hear from. We walk by the poor on our streets and have no time to listen to them or be outraged by the injustices they have faced. The poor are voiceless in many ways. The meek are just that, meek. They find it hard to get a word in. The quiet people tend to get overlooked and drowned out by all the noisy people and egotists and narcissists who tend to have their say. If you doubt this, just spend a day listening to the radio or TV and note who gets the airtime.

And with the bereaved, that's an entire other story. In the Western world we like our bereaved brothers and sisters to be decently stoical and quiet. We will do anything not to be disturbed by their tears and agony. It is uncomfortable for us. When we might need to cry out in agony, or repeatedly tell the story of a lost loved one, who is there to listen to them? We are likely to be pointed in the direction of a professional grief counsellor where the grief can be safely handled, and we don't have to listen to the pain of others. The more we medicalize grief and pay to have it sorted out, perhaps the less we hear the real story of what it is to be ripped apart by the separation of death.

Why on earth did Jesus cry when his friend Lazarus died?[3] Jesus knew Lazarus had gone to glory. And yet he wept like the best of them. He could not remain silent in the face of such suffering. He himself gave voice in his tears to the story of loss beyond loss. Jesus was not married. He had no wife and children. And so the death of a friend hit him especially hard. God seems all the more human for it.

Perhaps being open to the stories of those who are not normally courted could be a focal point for the ministry of church. Where better to tell the stories of our ups and downs, triumphs and disasters than church? Church is a place not just where we can be real with God. It can also be a place where we make space to listen to and keep the stories of the poor, the meek and the bereaved.

Postmodernism

We live in what is often referred to as a post-truth postmodern age. They are long words but in essence they describe what is quite a common modern perception of reality. Modern folk tend to be suspicious of any claim on absolute truth. Truth is conditional – you have your truth and I have mine. It is arrogant to say that my truth has more validity than yours.

The world as we find it is squeamish about asserting absolute truth, and that makes it tricky for Christians who assert that Jesus is the truth, the way and the life.[4] How can we hang on to the truth in a world of multiple truths? Especially as we don't want to seem arrogant and exclusive. Truth is a tricky area for us today.

There is a deep suspicion of metanarratives – big stories that explain everything, universal truths and explanations. Instead, a large number of modern people pin their faith on small stories and personal stories. In some ways this rediscovery of the power of individual stories is extremely positive.

We may have issues with postmodernism. We may say that many people are more modernist than postmodernist. But with postmodernism in the air, and cries of fake news abroad, this is surely an age when the personal story has gained more credence than ever before. If stories are more credible, then we have the chance to tell ours, and that is a strong and hopeful position to be in.

In some ways preaching has been infused with this same impulse. These days, sermons tend to be peppered with stories about families and partners and amusing anecdotes. Oral history is big news. All is not lost.

Our love of anecdote and personal story is an open door for us at church. It is a way of us connecting with the lives of those we serve. We are in the golden age of storytelling and story-listening. What we may need to do is to make sure that we have a way and a heart for hearing the stories of those whose voices have rarely been heard – especially in church.

Who gets left out?

An aside

Incidentally, there is another aspect of the post-modern critique of truth that rings true. The post-modernists argue that, when it comes to stories, the powerful always win and always get their voices heard. It is hard to disagree, although there are some shards of alternative storytelling. We know what happened in the Holocaust because we have the first-hand accounts. We know about other atrocities and examples of ethnic cleansing. Sometimes the victims do tell their tale, and when we hear it, we often react with horror.

But, in general, the victors and the strong always get to shape history by telling *their* story from *their* winners' perspective. The marginalized, the poor, the old and the refugee rarely get to claim history because their stories are too quiet and too weak. Stories are about power and the powerful always have the upper hand. That's what postmodernism asserts. There is clearly something in this.

This takes on a particular resonance when we think that Jesus told us that the first will be last in the kingdom of heaven.[5] If the stories of the last aren't being told or listened to now, then one day they will be centre stage. When the first are last, we will get to hear from them.

There is a wonderful story of the other Lazarus and the rich man. Lazarus is a beggar and covered in sores. During his life he is ignored by the rich man who passes him by.

> The time came when the beggar died and the angels carried him to Abraham's side. The rich man also died and was buried. In Hades, where he was in torment, he looked up and saw Abraham far away, with Lazarus by his side. So he called to him, 'Father Abraham, have pity on me and send Lazarus to dip the tip of his finger in water and cool my tongue, because I am in agony in this fire.'
> Luke 16:22–24

The rich man begs that his story is circulated to his loved ones so that they might be warned. Abraham refuses.

> He said to him, 'If they do not listen to Moses and the Prophets, they will not be convinced even if someone rises from the dead.'

The rich are deaf to the stories of the poor. Nothing will get them to take notice. In this life the powerful have developed a deafness and it's something we might take as a warning. Do we need to start the listening process right now?

It behoves us to begin listening. Especially if we pray 'your kingdom come . . . on earth as it is in heaven'[6] with any conviction at all. Then we usher a part of that kingdom in by hearing and making time to hear the tales of the weak, marginalized and poor.

By listening to the stories of the old, the weak, the marginalized, the poor and all the rest, we reclaim storytelling not for the victor but for the victim. And we do this in church as a matter of course. If we can't hear the defeated, the last and the poor, where can they be heard?

Two groups

There are two groups of people who, it seems to me, have the most difficulty in getting heard – and there are probably many others. These groups are the very young and the very old. I will leave discussion of the very young for another time.

The elderly often have no one to tell their stories to. If they do have, then people can be tired of hearing the same thing a number of times over. And yet, when one begins to hear reminiscences from elders, the richness and variety of them is amazing. The stories of these folk are alive with humour and tragedy and inspiration. I, for one, don't want to lose this. In fact, I want to hear more stories because I feel somehow that in them, I might learn something about myself, and about how to get through life.

Listening to others

When I was studying for ordination, we had one talk that has stuck in my mind. In it, we heard of a radical experiment of listening to stories and the disadvantaged.

Yvonne Richmond was a priest up north who was feeling that our existing strategies for mission and evangelism were no longer working. When praying about her future ministry, she felt God say to research spirituality outside of church. She spoke to her bishop who was willing for her to do this, and they came up with a plan.

Yvonne was to take a break with a purpose. She gathered a team to interview people about their spiritual experiences and understanding of church, and her discoveries revitalized her ministry. She found that people who never attend church were having supernatural experiences. They saw angels and had powerful experiences of Jesus, yet they found the church to be somewhere that didn't expect that of them. Spirituality outside church was growing while congregations shrank.

The people she interviewed trusted her. They trusted her with their stories. Yvonne realized that they showed something amazing: that the Holy Spirit is at work in the lives of people outside our churches. We need to take the time to listen to people we might not normally listen to, to see what God is doing and learn from them about him, and then explain their experiences, rather than think we have exclusive rights to God.

Yvonne said a very provocative thing to us students that went something like this:

> We shouldn't assume God needs us. God is revealing himself to people who are not yet believers and we need to catch up with what he is doing.

Well, this may be true, but it does ask of us some very challenging questions. If we want to hear the stories of the disadvantaged and the powerless, are we even in the right place to hear them? Perhaps we need to either get new friends, new places or step outside of the church and spend more time listening.

I go up to the local authority gym and I've found the locker room to be a fruitful place for hearing stories. People know I'm a vicar – the clergy clothes I turn up in and change out of are a good clue. But I have built up quite a group of guys who will say a cheerful 'Morning, Father'.

And when no one is looking and I'm having a cup of tea in the canteen they sidle up to me and speak about their lives and their problems and the wrestling they've had with faith.

It's not that the world is hostile to us; it's that we can be hostile and scared of the world. The world has stories to tell us, but can we be brave enough to hear them? Where is your place of contact?

One day a gym member asked me what I thought about life after death. It's a good question, and I replied with my normal, 'Why do you ask?' These kinds of questions tend to unlock a story or at least give a person permission to tell one.

It turned out that the fellow had recently lost his wife and was missing her terribly. Each day he spent half an hour looking at her picture and talking with her. He felt her presence everywhere in the house. He wanted to know if this was odd.

Study questions

1. *So, who gets to tell the best stories? Who should we actually be listening to? The Beatitudes begin to give us a clue.*

   Is it only the winners who get to tell their story? How do we hear the stories of the lost? Who would you consider in your community and church to be those who least get to tell their story? Is it the young, or the old, or the lost and the lonely?

2. *Perhaps being open to the stories of those who are not normally courted could be a focal point for the ministry of church. Where better to tell the stories of our ups and downs, triumphs and disasters than church?*

   What would church be like if it was like this? How does your church do? What kind of stories might you and your friends tell if there was space and time in church to tell them?

3. *By listening to the stories of the old, the weak, the marginalized, the poor and all the rest, we reclaim storytelling not for the victor but for the victim. And we do this in church as a matter of course. If we can't hear the defeated, the last and the poor, where can they be heard?*

Discuss. How does this make you feel and respond?

Prayer

Father, would you help us not to drown out the stories of the lost and the lonely? When we exultantly worship, help us to also find time for lament and listening. Help us to be sensitive and to open pathways that encourage stories we may be uncomfortable to hear.
Help us to be agents of change in our communities – sticking up for those without a voice.

PART THREE

Some Stories for Real

12

The Maître d' and the Gucci Shoes

Whoever has ears, let them hear.

Matthew 11:15

Stephen was the maître d' at L'Escargot restaurant in Soho in the 1980s. When the royal family were going to dine, he'd get a call and exchange a code word to make sure they had just the right table. He rubbed shoulders with pop stars and film stars. He was named in the press as one of the most influential people in London. Life was good.

'I wanted for nothing. I got a huge salary and never paid for things – meals, clothes, you name it, all were given to me,' Stephen explains.

It was the high life. Stephen made no secret that he was gay.

While Stephen led the gilded life, the life of influence, something much darker was happening out in the world. HIV had struck and people were beginning to die. What's more the public were scared and there was a backlash. People were afraid to go near people who had the virus.

One day a friend of Stephen's invited him to visit the newly opened London Lighthouse. The London Lighthouse was an independent AIDS hospice, initiated by Christopher Spence and his partner, and which opened against an incredible amount of opposition. There were demonstrations and the press raged.

The London Lighthouse was at the epicentre of the epidemic and was most notably supported and visited several times by Princess Diana, Dame Elizabeth Taylor and Sir Elton John.

The memorial garden contains the scattered ashes of many people who died at the Lighthouse. It was a place of hope but also incredible anguish.

Stephen got his usual cab from the West End. Inside he heard a story and saw a story that changed his life forever. He met people who were dying and he listened to them and he began to realize that this story had tremendous power.

As he left the Lighthouse to go back to the restaurant, he caught sight of his beautiful Gucci suede shoes. They would have cost more than a regular person earned in two months.

In an odd way the story he had been part of in the hospice and the shoes spoke into Stephen's life. He could no longer close his ears and his eyes and he had to make a change.

That change has been astounding.

I am right now standing with Stephen in the organization he founded – Laurence's Larder at a church in Brent. It is a soup kitchen, but with a difference. It takes all that Stephen has learned and puts it at God's disposal.

Stephen left that meeting and his destination with shoe-gazing and made some changes. He trained as an HIV counsellor at the Lighthouse. He went to San Francisco to work with HIV patients at the large municipal hospital there; having trained he was licensed as a hospital chaplain for the Episcopalian Church of the USA.

'I was often the only visitor people had,' says Stephen. 'Their families were scared to come, there was such a stigma and such fear.'

Laurence's Larder opens its doors during the week. There is a queue of people wanting to come in. When they come in they get something so beautiful and unexpected it takes their breath away.

Stephen offers fine dining – beautiful food, napkins and tablecloths. Everyone is Sir or Madam. He has clothes and suits and shoes that people can take with them. Everyone gets a meal they can make on the street so they don't go hungry later on.

There is something so biblical here. People are made to feel like kings and queens. Why? Because the last will be first in the upside-down kingdom of God.

Because it's a foretaste of the heavenly banquet[1] and because Stephen had the sensitivity to listen to the whispering of a story that unsettled him and made him wonder what he was doing with his life and whether God had other plans.

You don't need a referral to come in. Everyone is welcome and so everyone comes.

Stephen says, 'We train people to cook and we get chefs coming to see what we do. We have contacts everywhere and people volunteer. Everyone is welcome.'

It was those Gucci shoes that did it.

Stephen reflects that: 'God has somehow brought together everything in my life and allowed me to put it into this. I am 72. I understand catering and hospitality and I was an HIV counsellor. I am the son of a bankrupt and my dad served a prison term for embezzlement. We lost everything but most of all we were ashamed. But I'm not ashamed now.'

Stephen explains that God took down his defences: 'My excellent Armani suit and Gucci shoes were my uniform and my armour. The rich and famous saw me in them and thought they knew me. But inside was still the little boy Stephen, whose father had hurt him and his family so much.'

No amount of theology could have caused such a godly set of circumstances to arrive. What it took was to be open to a new story and to live out a new story as well. Stephen listened to the calling of his heart and a calling to make a difference. He was a Christian already, but the story connected him deeply with the social gospel – the desire to do good and be a blessing, no strings attached.

I received an email from some volunteers who came to our memory café this week. In it, they say how much joy they experienced among those with dementia and those who were working with them; they loved every minute and felt humbled by what they saw.

I feel humbled every week by the love I see from family members towards those who have dementia, and it can be very difficult. I am glad that our visitors felt humbled, but what were they humbled by?

Perhaps it was the sight of pure altruism and the pure love of servanthood. I wonder if this is a story that will speak deeply to our volunteers over the weeks.

> Perhaps it was the sight of pure altruism and the pure love of servanthood.

Who knows: it might be the equivalent of Stephen's funky shoes?

Study questions

Reflect on this story. How does it impact you and what do you take from it? The following quotes may help.

Stephen offers fine dining – beautiful food, napkins and tablecloths. Everyone is Sir or Madam. He has clothes and suits and shoes that people can take with them. Everyone gets a meal they can make on the street so they don't go hungry later on.

It was those Gucci shoes that did it.

Prayer

*Father, please help me to have my own 'shoes'
moment. I want to see where I am trusting in
material wealth and privilege and then to trust
in you. Give me the boldness to change direction
when I need to and to hear the cry of those who are
perishing.*

*Help me to acknowledge all my past failures and
regrets but not to be dominated by them. Let me
see them as part of the tapestry of my life, and –
with both the good and the bad parts – see your
hand in everything and your hope in my future and
the future of my community and church.*

13

The Street-fighting Man

We were therefore buried with him
through baptism into death in order
that, just as Christ was raised from the
dead through the glory of the Father,
we too may live a new life.

Romans 6:4

Lukey's a big fella. He's well over six foot and stocky. He's got a gentle Dublin brogue and looks you in the eye. He might be scary if he didn't smile so beautifully.

I got to know Lukey when I first became priest here at St Cuthbert's, North Wembley. One of my parishioners asked, 'Have you met Lukey yet?' with a twinkle in their eye. I hadn't.

Within a few seconds of meeting him I was enveloped in a hug that felt like a friendly old brown bear had got hold of me. As the months went on, I began to get to know Lukey's story. He asked me to tell it here.

Lukey grew up in the slums of Dublin with his eight brothers and sisters. The family moved to London and settled in Willesden – then a centre for the Irish community. His mum had a lot on her plate and Lukey went into an orphanage, along with seven of his brothers and sisters. The children were split up. It was a horrible experience – full of suffering – and Lukey lashed out. He was a fighter – he had to stick up for himself, no one else would.

Out of care, Lukey skirted with being on the right side of the law. He became a street fighter; he drank, took drugs and found work wherever he could.

He was tough, feared even, but he was a mess, and he knew he was a mess.

Lukey's gambling and frequent pub attendance led to his marriage breaking up and Lukey being home-less. He had an alcohol-induced breakdown and spent time in a mental hospital.

'I was on the way down and I couldn't stop myself. I lost everything,' he tells me.

After a meeting with a person who spoke about Je-sus, Lukey became a Christian. But he wasn't out of the woods. He still felt lost and angry.

After becoming a Christian, Lukey made friends with a couple. They were Christians and they let him come and see them when he felt bad. Gently, they coaxed his story out of him. They spent time listening to him and praying with him. They took a risk. It would have been so easy to smile and do a perfunctory prayer and move on. But these heroes were happy to invest in a man who needed love, unconditional love, in or-der to see the love God had for him too. Lukey was transformed. The events he had been through were still with him, but the pain subsided.

And what I had was a friendship with the big man. New into being a parish priest, I needed all the friends I could get. Every Sunday, Lukey was there, down the front smiling and encouraging me. The one fella who found my jokes funny and got me, understood me. Every vicar needs a Lukey. I found myself enjoying his company and able to share my ups and downs with him. He'd been through so much that a wisdom was upon him.

Lukey is a charismatic Christian, although he isn't one for labels. One minute he is full of jollity and aware of God and grateful. The next he might be wrestling with his demons – but then, don't we all?

One Sunday I was doing my talk at church and I felt a tap on my shoulder. It was Lukey; he'd come up to the lectern.

'Steve, can I say something?'

What was there to lose? I passed him the microphone which was something we were wisely counselled against during vicar training. 'Hang on to the microphone at all times,' was our collective call.

And then in near-silence from the congregation he told about his life. He spoke about the time he felt he could no longer go on and his life had stopped making sense to him. He spoke about the saints – the everyday people who had cared enough to let him be himself but to counsel him and pray with him and give him fresh hope.

He spoke into the lives of our people. It was amazing, really, and there was barely a dry eye in the house. His life story, told from the heart, was way better than my sermon. Indeed, it made me rethink the way I preached completely. I had a

> His story was pivotal in helping our church to discover something about God.

prompting to be more personal, direct and to really engage with where I was at and the people I serve were at.

Lukey took a risk. Lukey is bouncy Lukey – a kind of glorious Tigger, loved by all. It is easy to misjudge and underestimate people who are open and honest about themselves. But he has a story to tell and we were able to listen to it.

Lukey does not fight or gamble or drink any more. He has bad days and good days. His story was pivotal in helping our church to discover something about God and to see God in the everyday life of a brother.

In the months that followed, Lukey regularly came to the front to share a word with us or a story.

He backed it up by meeting all kinds of people on the streets and bringing them to church. They trusted him. We began to get homeless people turning up with Lukey, and those who had suffered with drug abuse and other addictions.

'I couldn't walk by people who I met. I saw their suffering. I understood them and they trusted me because I had lived the same story as them,' he says.

Lukey's people became our people and we, I think, began to find a new sense of direction and purpose. At least, that's how it seemed to me. The power of stories cannot be underestimated. In our church they opened us up and reminded us that there were many out there who were lost and also needed the help we have a real heart to provide.

Lukey has now moved north and is at a new church. He seems surprised that a pattern has reoccurred.

'It's amazing. The same thing is happening here. I'm meeting the lost and the broken-hearted and they are coming to church,' he says. 'I have become friends with an ex-Hell's Angel. I have a cup of tea with him every day.'

Of course he does.

Study questions

Reflect on this story. How does it impact you and what do you take from it? The following quotes may help.

He spoke into the lives of our people. It was amazing, really, and there was barely a dry eye in the house. His life story, told from the heart, was way better than my sermon.

Lukey's people became our people and we, I think, began to find a new sense of direction and purpose. At least, that's how it seemed to me. The power of stories cannot be underestimated. In our church they opened us up and reminded us that there were many out there who were lost and also needed the help we have a real heart to provide.

Prayer

*Father, we sometimes don't hear from those who
are on the margins and are hidden in plain sight.
We walk past the people who are being trafficked
or those who don't know when the next meal is
coming. Open our eyes and our ears and give a new
calling to really be a blessing.*

14

The Playwright and the Schoolboy

> The only people to whose opinions I
> listen now with any respect are people
> much younger than myself. They seem
> in front of me. Life has revealed to them
> her latest wonder.
>
> Oscar Wilde, *The Picture of Dorian Gray*

I'd completely forgotten about the letter.[1] It's not that surprising as I'd received it in February 1981. I was 18 and living with my parents in Northolt, west London. And for at least the last twenty-five years it has been in the garage in a box. Forgotten and unloved.

That was until we decided something had to be done about the mess and we had a good old sort out. My daughter found it and, handing it to me, asked, 'Who's this from, Dad?'

I knew who it was from the minute she gave it to me. It was from John Osborne, writer of *Look Back in Anger*.

As I said earlier, as a sixth former I'd read the play and loved it. I saw myself in the character of Jimmy Porter, the original angry young man. I remember that I was terribly unhappy when I wrote to John Osborne – problems at school. I had poured my heart out, wondering if there were any things worth fighting for and lamenting so much about being in a tough school and being the one kid who seemed to love books and stories.

I did something that I had not done before – I opened up about my story, my real story. I happened to do it to a stranger and a writer whom I admired. That stranger could very easily have ignored my letter.

I remember when the reply dropped through the letter box and my father handed it to me.

But seeing it now was more than just being back there in the family home. It was more than this. The letter was like a prophecy, a fortune-telling. It took me back in time to a very different me.

Turning it over in my hands I marvelled at the embossed address – Edenbridge, Kent and the all-caps simple header JOHN OSBORNE.

Somehow my letter created a strange bond with the playwright. In the first paragraph he tells me, 'Well, Steve, I am indeed alive – although a few years ago I'd begun to care little one way or the other.'

A precious exchange was taking place. My story had opened up his. It is unthinkable that a public person would answer in these terms today, perhaps.

Poignantly, he tells me that he has never felt more full of energy in every way. That he's almost looking forward to his future and that his work is going well.

That year saw the release of his first volume of autobiography, but soon after he'd be struck down with diabetes. And the plays had dried up. Of course, he died young and hugely in debt. His optimism may have been short-lived but that's where he was and he shared it with me – probably to cheer us both up.

As I say, I had lamented the lack of great and brave causes – Jimmy's great obsession. I wondered if there were any. He tells me not to take the line too seriously.

'It is a cry of anguish', he says. 'It's true but so was, "My God, my God why hast thou forsaken me." Surely the most terrifying utterance ever. To give voice to such things in despair is – or may be – another way of expressing defiance. Life is indeed bleak and grey and, like others, I have spent long, bleak and grey nights without hope, peace, love or kindness. Only cruelty and one's own desolation.'

As I say, can you imagine a celebrity author writing with such intensity and honesty to a schoolboy he had never met? The letter is laced with references to God and the way he has blessed Osborne over the years.

But then Osborne sets out to advise the young me, and he does so with great kindness, despite his reservations:

I have had a fierce sort of life – not merely inner – and my advice may have little value, but I was touched by the unusual openness of your letter.

He tells me:

> It takes a long time to discover that because of that very desolation, there may be fun, vitality and all sorts of comfort and delight.
>
> In the meantime get what you want without hurting others. Don't be too hard on yourself. Life will do that from what I can see in your letter. Don't be cheated of that 'grandeur and delicacy' you suspect is still there. It <u>is!</u>

At the time of the letter I saw myself as an atheist. Osborne tells me:

> You are probably 'religious' without being aware of it. You sound like it. It is no more than an awareness of the divinity of life and a belief that, in spite of all the lions, bureaucrats, schoolteachers, wayfarers, kings, deceivers and dissenters of all kinds, we do not have to be brutish and bullying like blind troglodytes. There is a world elsewhere. As dear Shakespeare said: 'there is a special providence in the fall of a sparrow.' Don't lose sight of it.

But there's more to come. As I sit here reading the letter it moves me tremendously. I have to say that it has made me cry in a way I haven't done for years. Why was I crying? I think it is because the letter and the story exchange made me feel sorry for the boy I had been. I was so terribly lost.

> The letter and the story exchange made me feel sorry for the boy I had been.

That Osborne would write to me and take such time to engage with my teenage angst was amazing. He had a premonition that I myself thought was nonsense at the time.

A few weeks later the phone rang at home. My father answered it.

'Son, fella on the phone says he's John Osborne, wants to speak to you.'

I walked gingerly to the foot of the stairs where we kept the phone. I can't remember the call but I know I was tongue-tied and embarrassed. I didn't know what to say to my hero. But I was grateful too. I know that Osborne asked me how I was doing and wanted to check that I was OK.

Over the coming years I would send him my poems. Heaven forbid! And he would send a kind card back encouraging me to write. I am sure that if he were alive now, he would be delighted that I had become a vicar – at one point in the letter he warns about the dangers of trendy vicars. I'm certainly not one of those.

It was years later that I spoke to my father about the call we got that night. He remembered it for good reason.

He was a Cockney and he had never been to the theatre. Well, he went once. My mother took him to see the original *Look Back in Anger* at the Royal Court Theatre in the first few weeks of the run. I wonder why on earth they went. Perhaps they had read about it in the papers. Mum was always trying to give Dad some new horizons.

He loved it. In fact he found the play funny and laughed a lot. Interestingly this was actually the response that Osborne was looking for – he thought it was a funny play too. But my dad embarrassed my mother because other people weren't laughing and they shushed him.

My father never went to the theatre again. I never took up John Osborne's offer of going with my dad to have tea with him. The letter sat in the garage. But the story started a subtle change in my life.

Study questions

Reflect on this story. How does it impact you and what do you take from it? The following quotes may help.

I did something that I had not done before – I opened up about my story, my real story. I happened to do it to a stranger and a writer whom I admired. That stranger could very easily have ignored my letter.

My father never went to the theatre again. I never took up John Osborne's offer of going with my dad to have tea with him. The letter sat in the garage. But the story started a subtle change in my life.

Prayer

*Thank you for the strangers who sometimes take
the time to listen and respond to us. We sometimes
feel a kind of despair and anxiety and when another
human being takes that seriously it can be a great
comfort to us.*

15

Holy Cow

The question is not, Can they *reason*?
nor, Can they *talk*? but, Can they *suffer*?

Jeremy Bentham, *An Introduction to the
Principles of Morals and Legislation*

Poet Jonathan Steffen imagines the great saint visiting a place of dread – the slaughterhouse.

> *St Francis in the Slaughterhouse*
> He left his sparrows waiting at the door
> And entered like a draught, his bare feet treading
> Silent on the wetness of the floor;
> And, lifting up his hand, approached the pen
> Where patiently his brothers waited for
> The second coming of the slaughtermen;
> And like a draught his love went over them.
> And they saw nothing but his upraised hand,
> Knew nothing but the death that it would bring;
> And looked, and waited for the blow to land.
> And silently, the men appeared, and swept
> The floor, and strewed it with an inch of sand.
> And Francis fell upon his knees, and wept.
> And like a draught his love went over them.[1]

If we took a step back to consider the plight of our animal friends, might we weep too? How could we tell their story and how might it change us and our attitude to the world we share with them? Might the story and a dose of empathy open us to a new experience of something that is very like wonderment and awe?

I was so taken by Jonathan's poem that I contacted him to find out more. I think that Jonathan was touched by my love for his poem, all the more so because the poem meant such a lot to him. His answer opens up something of the odd link between moments of despair and terror and occasional intimations of wonder. Sometimes when we fully see the potential for something very dark, the light comes through. It's something that John in his mystical gospel comes back to time and again.

Jonathan takes up the story of the odd agonized birth of his poem. For a start he imagined the scene of the saint and the slaughterhouse.

> I don't know if St Francis (one of my favourite saints) actually ever visited a slaughter-house – although, given the conditions of life in his day, he would certainly have been very familiar with the slaughter of livestock.

Jonathan was experiencing moments of the dreaded artistic block – even though he was surrounded by encouragement and help.

> I was on a Creative Writing Fellowship and was finding it very difficult to write in circumstances that were supposed to be ideal for writers.

The hospitality and generosity were marvellous, but I felt rather like a bird in a gilded cage, and I struggled to work on the project that I had hoped to complete. I would abscond whenever I could, going on long and solitary walks through the surrounding countryside.

It was a good tactic. It was one that the great William Wordsworth would employ. If you are stuck and sitting inside, get out into the natural world and see what happens.

On one of these walks, which took place in the late afternoon of a dull and overcast February day, I suddenly came across a small herd of cattle penned together by portable barriers. Standing around, but not directly involved with the cattle, were a number of men who did not appear to be farmers or farm hands. They seemed to be waiting to put the cattle in a large lorry that was parked nearby. But nothing was happening: the men were doing nothing, no-one seemed to be in charge, and the atmosphere, under an oppressively low and grey sky, was full of dread. I could sense what the cattle were feeling. Of course, I could do nothing about it. Eventually I moved on, but the experience stayed with me and would give me no rest.

The ominous feeling wouldn't leave the poet. One is tempted to recall the great bard of Manchester, Steven Morrissey and his band The Smiths and his plaintive call about creatures of beauty dying. That call led a whole generation to vegetarianism – contact with the creatures that God has made and the way we treat them sometimes does. Jonathan continues:

> Where I was staying had a very small library, and one of the books on the little shelf was a very formal and detailed introduction to prosody. I had been reading it for some time, during the hours when I should have been sitting at my typewriter in my room, writing short stories. The stimulus of this book, together with my recent immersion in the work of the German Czech poet Rainer Maria Rilke, combined with my experience of the cattle awaiting their fate, and the result was *St Francis in the Slaughter-House.*

The influence of a long-dead saint can have a huge influence on our experience not just of the faith but our own experience in the world that God has made. Jonathan simply placed the saint in a place of animal horror and let him do the rest – bringing out the odd awesomeness of love when all seems lost and hopeless. Jonathan adds:

I should mention that my father, who fought throughout the North African and Italian campaigns in the second World War, brought back with him an olive-wood carved bust of St Francis, which I still have, and which lives on my piano. I also attended a C of E school which instilled in me a very vivid sense of who St Francis was, and this was later amplified by studying Giotto's depictions of St Francis, as well as reading about his life and listening to some of his music. Ironically enough, my house in Cambridge used to be inhabited by Franciscan monks.

Our medieval forebears knew much about the power of the saints and it is a knowledge that we, by-and-large, have let slip. Or perhaps some of us haven't.

As for St Francis, he has always filled me with wonder – for his radical reconceptualisation of what it meant to live a life in imitation of Christ, for his courage and compassion, his love of animals and music, his energy and optimism, and his extraordinary skills as a communicator. Think of his invention of the Christmas crib with real animals, or his face-to-face attempt to convert Saladin in the midst of a Crusade.

This takes us back to the moment of connection with the animals of the field and their silent executioners. In a moment that has overtones of the cross, the poet and his muse, St Francis, realize that the death of these beautiful creatures is both tragic and full of wonder. Whatever we do to them, and whatever we did to the Christ, they will endure forever. Sometimes all we can do is look on in silent horror at what humankind can do and open ourselves to the redemptive power of love. That is so much more powerful than pure materialism and the world of selfish genes.

Christ's call of 'Father, forgive them, for they do not know what they are doing'[2] is a call of hope amid a moment of despair.

Before Jonathan returned to his writing and his own place of safety, he had one last job to do.

> I actually had something of a silent conversation with one of the cows, who was so beautiful that I understood for the first-time what Homer meant by the phrase 'the ox-eyed Juno.'

It is a numinous moment of true wonder because the cow is no longer an object, it has become a subject.

St Francis in the Slaughterhouse is soaked with the poignant love of a human being for his brother and sister creatures.

And Francis fell upon his knees, and wept.
And like a draught his love went over them.

Study questions

1. *If we took a step back to consider the plight of our animal friends, might we weep too? How could we tell their story and how might it change us and our attitude to the world we share with them?*

   How do we treat animals? How might our attitudes change?

2. *Before Jonathan returned to his writing and his own place of safety, he had one last job to do.*

   > *I actually had something of a silent conversation with one of the cows, who was so beautiful . . .*

   It is a numinous moment of true wonder because the cow is no longer an object, it has become a subject. St Francis in the Slaughterhouse *is soaked with the poignant love of a human being for his brother and sister creatures.*

   > *And Francis fell upon his knees, and wept.*
   > *And like a draught his love went over them.*

   Discuss.

Prayer

*Thank you for those moments when we suddenly
connect with the suffering and fear of the creatures
we share our planet with. Help us to reflect on how
we rely on them and how we should honour them.
We pray for those who work in the agricultural
industry. We ask you to fill us with the compassion
and closeness for all creatures that St Francis had.
May we also call them brother and sister and mean it.*

16

The Poet and the Asylum Seekers

Whoever oppresses the poor shows
contempt for their Maker, but whoever
is kind to the needy honours God.

Proverbs 14:31

Caroline Smith is an interesting artist – because she is both a poet and an immigration caseworker in Brent. She understands the value of stories in a professional work context and as an artist. She knows how to listen.

Each week she listens to many people who tell her how they got here and why. She may be the only person who hears that story and people may well be frightened to tell her what has happened. Asylum seekers fear that their story may sometimes lead to them being sent home and so they are often in a highly charged state.

We read so much in the media about this kind of issue, but Caroline is actually someone who hears first-hand what is happening.

Her recent collection, *The Immigration Handbook*, shows great empathy for those she works with and helps, and my conversation with her echoes so many of the themes in this book. It certainly speaks of the power of stories to move us and for us to see the real person and not the stereotype.

The starting point is that those seeking asylum are at the margins and sometimes fear telling their story. Caroline tells me:[1]

> It is important that we listen to the stories of those seeking asylum . . . so we can resolve their

problems. I've heard thousands of stories, and just the process of listening gives dignity and value to the lives of the tellers.

It is an important point. We confer dignity on another by actively listening to their life story. We assert that the person's life has value and they mean something.

> We confer dignity on another by actively listening to their life story.

But sometimes people are scared to tell the truth, especially if there are painful or what they see as shameful incidents. They are usually in limbo and are afraid of being deported.

Jesus often listened to people who were in limbo – the woman at the well, the woman with the issue of bleeding. The people he listened to had often felt that their future would just be more of the same as they already had. When people were stuck, meeting Jesus gave them fresh hope.

But Caroline sees a tremendously important role for art and for poetry. If we filter the stories we hear through poetry, then we tend to see them afresh. Art has a way of pointing us to the heart of an issue and giving us a fresh insight. Especially, poetry has a way of telling truth in a different way to journalism.

Art and poetry are at the heart of life. Whereas journalism alerts the public to issues, it can have a short attention span. But poetry is about choosing words very carefully. I didn't want my book to be polemic. Poetry allowed me to show the complex stories and the decisions people took – good and bad. Poetry gives you the whole person, and when you have that, you can have empathy.

And so Caroline spent five years writing the poems about the lives of those who have no voice, and the result captures something of what it is to be stateless and vulnerable. It is a window into a world that is somehow described more powerfully, perhaps, than by simple prose. Her poems have a beautiful rawness and capture the unfinishedness of people's lives. The gaps that poetry opens up allows the trauma and tragedy to speak through.

This poem is one of my favourites. Partly that's because I know the area it is set in very well. The North Circular is a stone's throw from my parish and I pass the flats that are mentioned regularly. I also love it because it is rather like a parable – and especially the Good Samaritan. It speaks of human kindness which is generally an antidote to bureaucracy. It begins with what appears to be political campaigning – the letter-drop. It's an everyday kind of thing, but it opens up a story that is compelling. It says that behind every nondescript flat on every nondescript day there may be a story of hope and heartache. In this case it is Abdul Rahman who has offered a sofa to his friend Xiang Lee for the past two years.

It would be easy to write off Abdul. He's a serial letter writer – the kind of person who could be written off as vexatious and eccentric. The master of the green ink letter – the kind of regular correspondent who tends to bombard their local MP. But behind the letters is a man who understands hospitality. And he has a story of a man called Ray Watkins who once, years ago, offered him a chance that changed his prospects and his life.

Heron Flats
As you push a leaflet through a letterbox
Abdul Rahman dashes out
to petition the case of Xiang Lee
who's been sleeping on his sofa
for the past two years.
You ease off the messenger bag
and sit and take tea with him
on the balcony. You know Abdul,
a serial letter writer in green ink.
He arranges mint leaves in glasses
and you watch them twist and melt
like fur caterpillars, as you sip
on this Sunday afternoon

up here where the North Circular
is constant as the ocean and
next door's finches,
dyed to the colour of flamingos,
squall in their rows of cages.
What you didn't know, was how
hard it was, when he first came
to England in 1964, to get a job
and how many letters he'd written
and how he'd got no replies and then
how, one day, he got an interview
for a position as clerk at TL Holdings –
and how, when he'd got there
he'd found three other candidates
all foreigners like him
and how his boss, Ray Watkins
had taken them all.[2]

Study questions

1. *Jesus often listened to people who were in limbo – the woman at the well, the woman with the issue of bleeding. The people he listened to had often felt that their future would just be more of the same as they already had. When people were stuck, meeting Jesus gave them fresh hope.*

   Can you think of a time you experienced fresh hope during a difficult situation? How did this change what you were going through?

2. *Art and poetry are at the heart of life. Whereas journalism alerts the public to issues, it can have a short attention span. But poetry is about choosing words very carefully. I didn't want my book to be polemic. Poetry allowed me to show the complex stories and the decisions people took – good and bad. Poetry gives you the whole person, and when you have that, you can have empathy.*

   How has either poetry or novels influenced your life? Do you have a favourite poem? Why does it mean so much to you?

Prayer

Father, it is almost miraculous that the power of art can open our eyes to the lives of others. Thank you for the poets in this world and for those who are there to hear the stories of frightened people who do not know where to turn.

The poem opens a door onto a quiet act of friendship and we celebrate it and hope to be people who similarly offer friendship too. If we can help, let us be helpers. If we can listen, let us be listeners. And if we can write, let us be writers.

PART FOUR

The Church
and Stories

17

A Church Changed by Stories

And let us consider how we may spur
one another on towards love and good
deeds, not giving up meeting together,
as some are in the habit of doing, but
encouraging one another – and all the
more as you see the Day approaching.

Hebrews 10:24–25

The lunch club

We had a lunch club for older people. Fewer and fewer were coming and it was really quite complicated to run. We had to get the lunch cooked and get crockery and cutlery out. It was a logistical tour de force and required a rota, a shopping trip and much moving around of furniture. And at the end, the job of tidying up took a good hour.

I sometimes wondered whether it would be missed if we closed it down.

But then I went to see the Scottish pastor I mentioned earlier, and it seemed that this might be a place where we could try something new and begin a quest for personal history. We recast the session with the name Daytimers. That described what we were and when we met and had a nice gentle ring to it. Our aim was to get some new folk to come and to add some vitality and energy to proceedings.

Our new group specialized in taking in people who were recently bereaved and rarely came to church. We had people who were a bit withdrawn although often stoical. Older folk have a remarkable resilience, but we all can be lonely and sad sometimes. Many felt that they had no one to talk to and that all they had lost was beyond telling to another human being.

Loneliness and grief are like distant countries. We suddenly find ourselves washed up in a place where our words have lost value and purchase. Trauma drives us to silence, and alienation pinches that silence so tight that it feels like we will never have language again. Sometimes language doesn't seem up to the job of digging us out of an emotional hole.

At Daytimers some people told me that these meetings gave them a chance to speak again in some profound way. The Christ on the cross doesn't deliver a sermon, and his words are few. And yet he articulates a basic human cry – he feels that God has deserted him.[1] This is perhaps the most terrifying and oddly comforting line ever written. Christ feels that God has stopped listening, and his desolate cry is a stand-in for each time we feel the same way.

If we are called, as we are, to help usher in God's kingdom on earth as in heaven, then being there to hear the cries of anguish matters. It also matters that we can hear and celebrate the stories of joy and fun and humour.

We began with tea and cake, but we moved on to something far more substantial. As people began to share their stories, we experienced a depth of fellowship that took us all by surprise.

Running the group

We put together a new structure. We would ditch the big dinner, which took time away from talking as a group. Instead, the curate (that was me) would make a cake each week, and we'd have tea and coffee. Thankfully, after some disastrous cakes from me, that duty passed to others more skilled than I. It was the third week of eating cardboard that encouraged a hero from the group to step forward and rescue us.

We began each session with refreshments, and then we had a twenty-minute slot where a different person each week would tell their life story.

We followed this with a song.

And then we had a short Bible study and discussion and then a good twenty minutes for more chat and gossip.

It had what I always look for in groups – pace and structure. We did an attractive poster and flyer with a picture of a slice of cake on it, which always seems to draw people in.

On the first week we had fifteen, and this grew to about thirty over the months. We found that people who were bereaved began to come, and this gave them a chance to talk about their loved one and bring in photos and reminisce.

The Bible study was vigorous, sometimes funny and full of insight. Some of the new people who came began to come to church on a Sunday. But what was most astounding was what happened with the story part of proceedings.

Many of the people who were at Daytimers had been coming to church together for decades. When the church had nearly closed, they had been the faithful few who had kept things going. Their children and grandchildren had grown up together. They had met at the school gates, helped with jumble sales and sung in the choir.

But oddly, they had never shared their life stories with each other. Perhaps it was British reserve or the structure of Sunday services and how busy they can get.

In the first week we heard an amazing story of a person who had helped to build Spitfires in the war. She described her love of being a school teacher and spoke about the joys and sadnesses of her life. She told us how much she loved teaching history and how her father had first got her interested in the subject. She remembered some of the children she had taught. It was truly moving. As she finished there was an odd sound. It was the sound of the others clapping. She told us that she had been coming to this church for thirty years and loved it. But she said that she knew nothing of the stories of the many people she had attended church with over those thirty years.

The church that gets to know each other's stories is a strong one. It helps us to understand what makes us tick.

We were fortunate to have a great start. And we went from strength to strength. That first story was so open and honest, funny and moving that it emboldened others. In the end people were asking when it was their turn.

We heard from an army officer about the challenges of his time while on active service. He also talked to us about his very different experiences while working as a civilian.

Another had been the 'astrologer' on a Sunday newspaper and had once met an angel in a near-death experience.

There were fresh delights each week. And, as more of us told our stories, even the shy people wanted to join in. Each week we felt closer to each other, and when we prayed for one another the prayers took on a reality about people's lives that really counted. The questions were perceptive and helped those who told their stories to amplify certain parts. The way I would describe it is that the stories broke the ice. And that ice had silently held people for decades – as acquaintances, but not brothers and sisters in the faith.

Eventually it struck me that these people who I thought were such close-knit disciples had, in fact, known virtually nothing about each other. And I now think that this is probably true in every church in the land. I wonder if everywhere people don't really know much about the folk they sit next to on a Sunday.

What formed over the months was way more than a tea and coffee club. The Bible study became very personal – with people being much more real about the challenges they had with their faith. They could do this because they had entrusted each other with their personal stories. We encouraged a culture of letting people speak and really welcoming their insights.

The pastoral core of the group developed. People swapped numbers and, if someone was sick, another member of the group would follow them up. They organized lifts for each other. If they heard of a lonely neighbour or friend, they invited them along to Daytimers knowing that they would be in safe hands with us. People were happy to come along and bring people they cared about.

For me as the curate I began to look forward to Day-timers. It was the highlight of my week. As the days ticked by, I began to get ready and to anticipate what would happen this week. One Sunday in church the Daytimers group did most of the stuff at the ser-vice – they sang and did the talk and the reading.

And I began to realize that telling stories is the gate-way to evangelism and community. When we started an Alpha course, many of the Daytimers' gang came along. They came because Alpha didn't seem scary as eating and chatting already seemed quite nor-mal – it was what we already did at Daytimers!

When I moved on, I wondered what would happen to Daytimers. I had been leading it for a few years and was deeply associated with it. It was my baby. I am glad to report that, many years on, Daytimers is still going strong. The format is still pretty much the same and the storytelling continues.

The group had another function. Daytimers made a strong and positive statement that elders mattered to us.

I put it this way – personal histories played a part in our church. We saw how wonderful was the God who had given us such incredible lives and we began to be grateful and feel that our stories mattered.

Harper Lee in *To Kill a Mockingbird* has her hero Atticus Finch expound what has become a great descriptor of empathy. Finch says that we need to inhabit the lives of others and understand what makes them tick. If we do so, we understand their troubles and the way that they are. It is a great definition. I often remind myself to understand other people before I become impatient with them.

In a similar discussion group held at another church, one person told us of the pain she felt when a loved one died. She told us about all the happy times she had had, the trips she had gone on, what it felt like to be happy and how she had had a wonderful life. But loss is loss. And when we lose someone who is a big part of our life, it leaves a terrible gap. The heart cannot be ignored. Her story was touching and helped us to understand what it feels like when a person, who feels so close that they are part of us, dies.

There was not a dry eye in the house, but there was also a great deal of understanding. Many of us knew what it was to be in love with another person, and we could step in her shoes a little. I think we also appreciated both her honesty and courage. When a relationship that close ends so suddenly, who would not be shocked and stunned into a kind of deadly silence.

But we also appreciated how our friend had carried on and had not given up on God and how she had become such a great encourager to others. Her experience of loss had also helped her to be a great listener.

Her decision to open up to us had another effect. Spurred on by her simple honesty and unaffected style, others began to speak.

Jean Vanier in *Becoming Human*[2] captures the trajectory of this kind of honest sharing. As we understand ourselves, so we understand others. It helps us to be realistic about ourselves and those we share our lives with.

The idea of confronting reality is interesting. Our friend's description of the pain of love and the riskiness of it is a long way from the picture we see painted so often. By experiencing something of her profound loss we also ask ourselves questions like – is love worth it?

We also heard from a teacher who missed her colleagues but still received letters from some of the girls she had taught. We heard from someone who had helped to build tanks during the war. Another person told us about her daughter, the trials of being a mother – and the joys.

I wonder what it would have been like if we had not shared stories. I think that the church would have been spiritually poorer.

We received a great deal less resistance to change when those who were at the sharp end of it felt listened to and valued. We can be bolder about the future when we have told our stories of the past. And it was great fun. Who wouldn't enjoy hearing tales of past adventures and of what things used to be like? It helped us all to realize how we had adapted so well to a very different world.

It also opened up new possibilities for volunteering. Older folk, who have held positions in the church in their younger days, can begin to feel surplus to requirements.

One lady told me that she had always been involved in church and loved the place and the vicar. She was a rock. I spent a few hours at her flat drinking tea and taking time to listen to her story. Her contribution

I heard about the church and the cycles it had been through and its triumphs and disasters.

to the church over the years had been astounding. I had no idea! I heard about the church and the cycles it had been through and its triumphs and disasters.

I asked her to be my assistant. I said that I would pick her up every week and I wanted her to help to greet people, make them feel at ease and be a linchpin. I realized she was someone who wanted to be loved and wanted to be useful.

Every week I picked her up in my car and we'd chat about the news and politics. I saw a huge change come over her as she became much more positive about herself. She was simply a delight and became a flagbearer for all the work the church was doing. As the weeks went by, I began to look forward to our chats, and she became more and more animated – even funny. It just needed a little care and attention and listening to her story.

Study questions

1. *Trauma drives us to silence and alienation pinches that silence so tight that it feels like we will never have language again. Sometimes language doesn't seem up to the job of digging us out of an emotional hole.*

   Discuss. How does trauma drive us towards silence?

2. *In the first week we heard an amazing story of a person who had helped to build Spitfires in the war. She described her love of being a school teacher and spoke about the joys and sadnesses of her life.*

   What kind of amazing stories have you heard? Give some examples and explain how this made you feel.

3. *Eventually it struck me that these people who I thought were such close-knit disciples had in fact known virtually nothing about each other. And I now think that this is probably true in every church in the land.*

   Do you agree? Discuss. How would your church be changed by stories and taking the time to listen to them?

Prayer

Father, we revel in the varied lives of those we share church with. There is no such thing as an ordinary person, and when we hear stories and encourage fellowship then we begin to feel better about life and the world you have made for us. Help us to offer warmth and hope to those around us and see your wonderful work in the lives of others. Let us be childlike in our fascination with the world and the odd and wondrous beauty of those we are surrounded by.

18

Stories and Prayer

I pray that the eyes of your heart may be enlightened in order that you may know the hope to which he has called you, the riches of his glorious inheritance in his holy people . . .

Ephesians 1:18

Perhaps you feel a bit uneasy about all this talk of stories. It may feel voyeuristic and a bit odd to just collect stories. Sometimes the stories are so heartrending that we feel duty-bound to respond. Often the story is accompanied by a request for prayer – and that can be more than hard when the situation seems hopeless.

> Often the story is accompanied by a request for prayer – and that can be more than hard.

Sam Wells in a recent article[1] has outlined just such an issue. Interestingly, he highlighted the kind of issue that I myself have come across almost exactly. A friend tells you that her dad is in the later stages of dementia and explains just how hopeless it all looks. 'Pray for my dad, please,' she asks.

But what do you pray? The conventional kind of prayer is what Wells calls a resurrection prayer. In other words, you pray for the dad to be restored. You pray for a miracle. But you know that dementia only ends one way.

There's a second kind of conventional prayer – Wells calls it the prayer of the incarnation. In this kind of prayer we acknowledge the incarnation – that God suffered along with us and as one of us. We ask him to be with the person who is suffering, to give them patience to endure their suffering and to surround them with people who love them.[2]

The friend who came in desperate need is really asking for you to help her and her family to feel less alone.

Wells suggests that there's a third type of prayer – he calls it the prayer of transfiguration. This is how it goes. In this we ask for pain and suffering to be transfigured, to be seen in a new way and experienced in a new way. It is a prayer for ongoing grace and transformation in the way things are experienced – seeing suffering in the light of eternity.

Is it possible to redeem dementia or any other impossible situation? Is it possible to see something that is transformed but not destroyed? The transfiguration prayer holds out a kind of hope that I have seen lived out here at St Cuthbert's. Dementia is not the end of all hope.

I have seen so much heroism and selflessness and glimpses of joy in dementia that I feel we can see some of God's glory in it. Dementia is an evil thing, a desperate thing, but God's radiance can even shine in this story and in our prayers for those who are on this journey.

I have seen families come closer to God in the midst of losing a loved one day by day. Loved ones have told me that they have come to see unexpected moments of humour in dementia, that they have come to know that their loved one is still the same although they have been altered. They experience calm along with the rage and pain and suffering.

They have accepted the road that dementia has led their father or mother or sister or brother or friend or partner on. And in that dementia journey, they have also seen their loved ones transfigured in some mysterious way.

Their loved ones have dignity and glory somehow even in the midst of forgetting who they are. God holds their stories even when they have forgotten them and have begun to forget the person they were.

Staying there

When we hear the stories of pain offered to us, we aren't called to simply be recorders of those stories. Ben Quash in his beautiful book *Abiding*[3] highlights the essential issue of being listeners but also being those who stay and pray and care, even when things get difficult.

If a person tells us their story, if they face a situation that seems impossible, then just knowing that we will not go away is powerful.

When I was suffering from depression and anxiety, it was a lifesaver that I knew that my family would not desert me. Even though I told the same story of how I was feeling over and over again, they listened, and in knowing that they would be normal even when I wasn't, I got the courage to carry on.

Quash points out that we know little about the first thirty years of Jesus' life. But without that time Jesus would not have been the leader he was. He learned from those around him. He was part of a normal community – part of its banter and storytelling and ideas. He learned a trade, served customers and he was shaped by his family and community.

He ate, he drank, he slept, and he became the leader and saviour he was, shaped by ordinary life with ordinary people. That is the marvel of the incarnation.

In John's Gospel (chapter 10) the writer relates Jesus' story of the false shepherds – those who desert their sheep. The true shepherd, of course, never leaves. It is a model.

I have been struck by the times I have visited those who are dying; they don't particularly want me to say anything, they just want to know that I won't be hurrying off.

Study questions

1. *If a person tells us their story, if they face a situation that seems impossible, then just knowing that we will not go away is powerful.*

   How does hearing others' stories help you to pray for them? What kind of prayers might you have and offer?

2. *I have been struck by the times I have visited those who are dying; they don't particularly want me to say anything, they just want to know that I won't be hurrying off.*

   Discuss. How does simply being present help others?

Prayer

Father, we want to be faithful and to be present for our brothers and sisters who share our world with us. Help us not to rush off too quickly. Allow us to be a comfort and to help those in trouble to know we will not desert them and nor will you.
If we are in trouble and lonely, bring people to abide with us and help us to see your love in the love they have to offer us.

19

The Church That Forgot Itself

Then Jesus told his disciples a parable
[The Parable of the Persistent Widow] to
show them that they should always pray
and not give up.

Luke 18:1

Every community, every church has a story to tell. It will be a story of triumphs and defeats and peopled with characters. This story is precious. It tells something of the angle of travel of the church and the way God has been at work.

Sometimes the stories of a church – its history – are captured in official booklets or on websites. I am struck by how these official versions so often seem not to get to the real essence of a place. Sometimes a church just needs to be reminded of its unofficial history to get a new perspective.

A priest in a city-centre parish tells me that just this thing happened where she is. She was new and was trying to get a picture of her new place. She asked at services and emailed her parish to request that they send her stories – stories of the people who had come over the years and made a difference. There was a deafening silence.

A while later the priest met a stalwart of the church while doing her shopping. The stories came thick and fast. There was the long-time parishioner and churchwarden who had been a tower of strength. There was the person who had set up the pensioners' club and come every Friday, rain or snow, for thirty years. There was the organist who used to fall asleep mid-song and liked a sherry or two.

With the stories, the place came to life. It was like a well-written novel. But why had my friend's congregation been so silent? She decided to ask a few of them.

'We didn't think you'd be interested in that kind of story,' some told her. It was also a strong comment on what makes the story of a place. Is it the dates the building was put up, the name of the firm that built the organ and the day the Queen visited? Or is it the many tiny micro-stories of who was there and who made a difference, however small?

I think the silent response was when my friend realized just what a tough job she had taken on. She would need to invest in some storytelling and honouring of the heroes of the past.

The church that remembered

I began my faith life in a Pentecostal charismatic church planted from South Africa in the lecture hall of a medical school in a west London hospital. It was, and still is, exhilarating. I owe a great deal to this church.

Like many churches with this spiritual practice it was a beautiful noisy affair on a Sunday. There was a band and lots of singing and ecstatic worship. But the thing I most remember isn't all the stuff that happened during worship times – the immediatism of worship.

One week our pastor talked about the past and the story of the church. He reflected on the humble be-ginnings of the church. He and his wife arrived in London with little more than a backpack and a dream to lead a church in 'the greatest city in the world'. This turning point was one of the key stories the church often celebrated. It was a founding narrative. But there was another, less well-known, story to come.

In the very early days of this church, Sundays were a logistical nightmare. The church was in small prem-ises; it had nowhere to store anything and had to set everything up each week from scratch.

Our pastor spoke about two obscure people who had made a difference. They were elderly, but they had a car. Every Sunday they moved the church drum-kit, which they stored in their small and cramped flat, down three flights of stairs and brought it to church. They then packed it into their small car at the end of the service and took it all home again. They did this for years without complaining.

Without them, the service would have been flat. Who knows if things would ever have taken off with-out that kit and that sacrifice?

At the time, I wasn't quite sure why I found that story so powerful. But I think I know now. On the one hand it broadened the official narrative – the leaders' early struggles. But also it told the story of the church perfectly.

That church was full of people who had made a difference. They didn't do the glamorous stuff or public things. But they quietly built the kingdom of God, and in telling their story, the church saw its trajectory. Or perhaps more completely, it saw the trajectory that God had been on. One small story spoke loudly – and it warmed the hearts of those who listened, giving them hope and courage for the next step that the church was venturing onto.

Story timelines

Vaughan S. Roberts in *The Power of Story to Change a Church*[1] makes a passionate argument for churches to find out their story – to plot their narrative, and to do it in an intentional way, as part of a process. Without knowing the plot, it is hard to move a church on. It is part of helping a church to start to tell a new story. When we know the foundational story of a church – the story it tells about its origins – then we know what can come next. If a church can tell its story together and listen to the pieces that make the jigsaw, then it can start to build a new identity. You need to know how you got to where you are now in order to have any clue about where to go next.

The collecting of the unofficial history and story of a place can be done with intentionality and as part of the regular life of a church.

For two years I shepherded a church that was recovering from the death of its priest, who had been with them for four decades. I was an interim minister, so my role was to help the parish to be ready for the next part of its story.

The parish was missing its vicar greatly. When a patriarch leaves the scene of battle, the troops do not know which way is up and which way is down. One of my roles was to find out what kind of vicar should come next. After such a long period with the same vicar, there were also questions about where to head next. It can be a very daunting period when the security of a long-term incumbent comes to an end. It is almost as though the church is without a father or mother.

The church needed a fresh vision and sense of purpose. There were some exciting times ahead – a new story was about to begin to unfold. But in order for that story to take shape, and as a way of making peace with the past, the story of what *had been* needed to be told first.

In the flurry of the new, it is sometimes hard to see what has already been, and to see how that rich story might be an encouragement and warning for the future.

We had two experienced priests come to help us with this period. They helped us to relax a little. One of the first things they did was to get the church council and members of the congregation to reflect on the past. They posted up flip-chart sheets around the church walls each with dates on them – stretching through the decades.

They then challenged us to write up memories and significant happenings along this precious timeline. The aim was both to understand our history and to realize how many milestones there were to celebrate. We literally saw our history come together before our eyes. The church had become static, and the story it told was of decline. But was that the real truth? It seemed not.

Over the days and weeks, people began to use Post-it notes to add memories and thoughts. We stuck photos of people who had been significant in the life of the church on the walls. People began to remember the saints and be thankful for them. This was useful because it helped the church to see beyond the long-serving vicar who had reigned here. It helped the church to reclaim the forgotten stories and the forgotten saints.

We began to see patterns – the influence of the Windrush generation of people from the Caribbean, the various building projects, the sudden spurts of evangelistic activity and some of the lulls and challenges.

One of the foundational positive events that came up time and again was Billy Graham's incredible events at Wembley Stadium. You can see the stadium from the church and it dominates the area. During the Billy Graham years, the church took on a fresh outpouring of the Holy Spirit. It was one of the big events and parts of the life of this church.

Some people who were near the end of long lives managed to help us to fill in gaps very far back. We began to see just how faithful so many people had been. We saw changes in demographics and changes in the way the church saw itself in the community. We began to see some of the challenges the long-serving priest had gone through and some of the missteps along the way. None of the missteps proved fatal, which said something about the resilience of this amazing church.

After a month or so we had a story. There were gaps and times when no one could really remember what had happened. As people looked at the story, many felt gratitude for what had been done in the past. Some, of course, felt pain. Any story that doesn't paint the full picture cannot have real power.

Some of the painful incidents and times called for us to gather and pray and, yes, repent. But that story-fuelled repentance was part of the process of healing. It was healthy and a good sign for the church. This isn't an easy thing to do and is not a miracle cure, but it is a way of owning what has been – all of it.

We had an official history of the church that had been put together a few decades earlier. If you read it you would learn about the architecture and some of the changes in the church. But if you only read that, it would have been like seeing holiday snaps and thinking that the holiday was the story of the whole of our life and not just showing the best side for the camera.

The official history was surface, but the unofficial history stuck on the walls of this old church told something a great deal richer. It was the story of the people of God in this place, during this time.

The 'history' exercise had a number of perhaps un-expected outcomes. The congregation began to be a lot more positive about the church and stopped focusing on the recent troubles. They began to see that the church had been hugely robust. They also began to see the church as a community and not just a series of events or a parade of powerful influencers.

The unofficial history became a fresh story that could be retold and owned by the present congregation. A huge amount of fondness poured out for those who had been part of the journey of the church. People could see patterns emerging – they could see where the church had surged and where it had struggled, and this was a useful reminder of what to do and what not to do next. The church had grown when an evangelistic outpouring had developed during a Billy Graham crusade. It had grown when new migrants to this country had made their home in the church.

The communal telling of a story and sharing of memories had served to start a fresh page in the story of the community. What made it so effective was that it felt safe – it wasn't about criticism of individuals; it was about a more reasoned and

The communal telling of a story and sharing of memories had served to start a fresh page in the story of the community.

fairer appraisal; it created the ground of making a new community – of remaking the community that existed.

Community storytelling in Bible lands

The society that Jesus knew would have used stories to help to keep its past alive and to help people know who they were. Kenneth E. Bailey explains that in the south of Egypt, in the Lebanese mountains and in isolated communities in upper Syria and Iraq, life has remained largely unchanged since the time of Jesus. The communities have lived in a kind of splendid isolation from the rest of the world.[2]

Even in 1983, when Bailey's book was published, many of these villages had not even a road to the outside world. He reports that they are like the tribes of old and retain their sense of identity through communal storytelling. Stories preserve what is important about their life together. In these communities, men gather each night to hear the old stories faithfully told. The stories are a way of maintaining the community, of giving it hope and a sense of identity.

Stories are more than entertainment; any society knows that. In the remembering and retelling of stories, a society hangs onto what it has been and what it is. To forget them is dangerous.

When the people of Israel in the Bible remember and retell their story with God, then they see a way forward. The story gives them fresh hope and direction. When they forget their story, then disaster has a habit of striking.

We see time and again the remembrance of the miraculous release from captivity. It is the central communal memory, and it forms part of the crucial insight that 'You are our God and we are your people'.[3] God himself frequently reminds the Jewish people of their story with him. It is precious and a building block for community.

There's an interesting point here, of course. Jesus takes the official story of his people – the plotline of their release from captivity and favoured status. He takes the official story and adds a new twist – a new way of looking at things.

He adds a powerful fresh strand of narrative with him, the cross and the resurrection. It is this that so scandalizes the people who were comfortable with the story that they already had and owned. It was dangerous storytelling and Jesus paid for it with his life.

Study questions

1. *Our pastor spoke about two obscure people who had made a difference. They were elderly, but they had a car. Every Sunday they moved the church drum-kit, which they stored in their small and cramped flat, down three flights of stairs and brought it to church.*

   Can you think of stories like this? Who have been the unsung heroes of your church and why?

2. *The official history was surface, but the unofficial history stuck on the walls of this old church told something a great deal richer. It was the story of the people of God in this place, during this time.*

   What is the unofficial history of your church?

Prayer

Hallelujah to all the unsung heroes. The people who washed up, turned up, set things up and stacked the chairs. The people who offered a helping hand. The people who got up early and stayed late and gave us a smile when we needed it.
Let me be an unsung hero – to avoid the lure of being at the front and on display.

20

Last Word

Whether I shall turn out to be the hero of my own life, or whether that station will be held by anybody else, these pages must show.

Charles Dickens, *David Copperfield*

There are no ordinary people

C.S. Lewis isn't really known for his sermons. In one of the earliest he preached, he makes a startling, though simple claim.[1]

The vast majority of it is philosophical in nature and I suspect that some of the folk listening to it may have found it hard-going. Towards the end of the sermon, Lewis changes gear and says he is about to offer something practical for his listeners. His insight is that there is no such thing as an ordinary person.

Lewis has a finely tuned sensibility for heaven and the alternative. Either glory or horror awaits each of us. If this is true, those we share the earth with now need to be taken very seriously – for one day we may spend eternity with them.

Each of us, one day, will be creatures of such glory or horror that we cannot comprehend. At the end of our lives we will be transformed either into glory or not. In this case there is no such thing as a mere mortal – everyone will be immortal – in one destination or another.

If this is true, then even the dullest person we meet is worthy of huge attention, love and listening-to. What they are is not what they will become.

C.S. Lewis and storytelling

C.S. Lewis loved fairy stories and his colleagues made fun of him for it. He read them his whole life and when he read an early draft of *The Lion, the Witch and the Wardrobe* to J.R.R. Tolkien, Tolkien didn't like it much. Lewis pressed on.

It seems a bit odd that this learned professor only began writing children's stories when he was in his fifties – a childless bachelor, who grew *into* allowing himself to be a bit more childlike. What seems clear, is that Lewis loved writing them because he knew that stories could do more than just convey meaning or explain how things worked – they were a window onto a deeper appreciation of the world, they were the way that we solved mysteries.

It's right at the end of the Narnia series that we get a startling piece of text.

The great story

The Narnia adventures are nearly over. It becomes obvious that the children are facing the next step of a journey that goes beyond the grave.

Aslan, the great God in lion form, has the job of somehow summing up. It is time to bring the threads together and end the narrative. Aslan has something very important to usher into being – the rest of the story.

> All their life in this world and all their adventures in Narnia had only been the cover and the title page: now at last they were beginning Chapter One of the Great Story which no one on earth has read: which goes on for ever: in which every chapter is better than the one before.[2]

For us, the readers, this is the end of the adventure – the end of all the stories. But we are reassured that they will live happily ever after. Isn't that what we all want for those we love? Lewis assures the reader that truly, at the end of the great narrative of our lives, things so beautiful are in store that they are beyond human language.

But what about the Pevensie children and their friends in the Narnia story? What of them? The children's lives had just been like the cover of the book and the title page. What seemed like a long time and an entire life was just the merest start of things.

Now they, as we in our turn will, start the great story of existence. Each chapter will be greater than the last, and the book never ends. Few of us can resist this calling to the deep yearning of our hearts. Even the most hardened of atheists, when presented with the possibility of heaven, might find it hard to resist.

Lewis acknowledges that we are 'here today and gone tomorrow' people. That for millennia after our own deaths, things will go on. Our time here is just the title page and the front cover.

This, in itself, is a healthy corrective to any hubris we might fall into. The archives are full of once-famous people who no one has heard of any more. Indeed, most of us cannot even name our own family members from just a few generations ago.

What is perhaps most surprising is the way that Lewis deals so openly with death, especially in a children's book. He specifically links the great story of a life with the end of it. We perhaps could learn from this to take our own mortality a bit more seriously.

For Lewis, one detects a parallel between the great Lord of the universe and his creativity, and the act of our own story-creation. In some small way we emulate and celebrate God by being storytellers, just as he is. The imagination is baptized by stories and we become more fully realized as people. Or perhaps it is better to say that our imaginations are a component of our holiness – the baptized imagination, alive with God, is capable of stories that are so stirring that we have to read on.

It is interesting how many specifically story-like metaphors and phrases there are in the early chapters of Genesis. God speaks the universe into existence – he says, 'Let there be light'.[3] Our first father is given the task of naming the creatures – just as a novelist might name their characters. And, of course, God makes an appearance in his own authored-creation. The Christmas Story is a story of God the author stepping into the pages of the great story of life.

The incarnation is the story of God who has a major plot role and who is needed to bring about the defeat of evil and the saving of the world. That he does it with the help and accompaniment of humans, and angels and animals, shows that we are all caught up in the great story. While here, Jesus had one precious life, and he used it well.

The good news is a story with a happy ending. As we remember this it gives purpose to our own lives. But above all, Lewis' use of language is a whisper that storytelling might be part of the stuff of life as well as simple entertainment. If the whole of our lives – both before and after death – are a story (they have a beginning and a middle and an ending) then we honour the storyteller and begin to see our lives as narrative, as well as a set of scientific processes and interactions.

If our lives are part of the great story, then this encourages us to be storytellers and to listen to others' stories. If those who seem insignificant or unloved have a part of that great story, then we are duty-bound to listen. It also behoves us to open up with our own narratives. We can all choose to be a closed book.

We can all choose to stay quiet, but when we see storytelling as the stuff of life and faith, then we begin to truly want to speak.

Storytelling is what makes us human

It sets us apart from the rest of creation. It is a gift that we sometimes don't take advantage of – especially when we grow up. I can see no good reason why we shouldn't be like children – awestruck in the world of the imagination.

God spoke the world into being and the power of his imagination is what sustains us still.

So, can we find room for stories – room for personal histories and for constructing community histories too?

I do hope so.

I sometimes wonder if, when we meet Jesus, he will ask us whether we took time to listen to each other. He might ask whether we told our story and provided a place to hear other people's, and in these stories saw his mighty work.

I feel that he might be pleased if we took time to hear the stories of those who are frequently kept silent. In doing this we honour them and him. We show that each person is precious and that means that their lives are, and have been, precious too.

Jesus came to save us – not to save an idea. If we matter that much, then so do our lives and the stories we weave around us. God is right in the middle of the stories. Perhaps one day you will tell me yours.

Jesus came to save us – not to save an idea.

APPENDIX

Practical Tips for Becoming a Storytelling Church

So, what could you do at your church and in your community to encourage an outbreak of personal history-telling? There are so many ways that this evangelistic and pastoral ministry can come to life and each will be personal to you.

Perhaps it starts with the insight that people's stories matter – that life is given shape by them (they give us a sense of an ending) and that in the telling of them and listening to them, we build confidence that the tellers are ultimately so precious to God that Jesus died for them.

At its simplest, Jesus gave his life so that we could have the kind of lives we tell others about, and so that they have ears to hear.

Perhaps also it is good to be clear about some of the benefits of encouraging stories. With the sharing of stories comes a great sense of family, and when the church feels like family, it seems to gain confidence in sharing the faith. What's more, if a church becomes known as a place where people can be at home and be themselves, it becomes a rather attractive proposition.

More on Daytimers

Daytimers is a very simple group to set up. All you need is a cake, some tea and coffee, Bibles and a warm room. It helps to run it every week so people get into the swing of coming. It helps also to have the same leader as people begin to feel in safe hands. A warm welcome at the door always helps and getting to know each other's names is vital. It is always a shock to discover the incredible impact of hospitality.

At each session we encourage people to speak for just ten minutes or so about their lives. As the group grows, spread the good news about it and talk about it at your Sunday service. Pray for it as a church. See it as a crucial new congregation and evangelistic and pastoral outreach. Celebrate highlights and encourage people to come along.

Encourage people to start volunteering. Widen the circle of cake-makers. Encourage people to act as welcomers and befrienders. See if someone might act as a driver to bring those who might find it hard to get there otherwise. Get different folk to read the Bible passage each week.

The key is to let the group take its own shape and to be a place of hope and safety.

Pray each week specifically for the needs that come up. When a prayer is answered, acknowledge that. Share out the leading of the Bible study. It doesn't matter if sometimes you go a bit off-piste. Instead, study the Word lightly, encourage personal insight and stories about the passage. Encourage people to get involved, and never correct them in public. As people get more and more comfortable with this style of Bible study, they tend to be more prepared to discuss issues in their own lives.

The most important thing at Daytimers is fellowship and belonging, and everything else follows on from this. The sense of belonging helps people to tell their stories and begin to enjoy the stories others have to tell. They join in, and the magic of weaving stories helps people to see connections between each other and to look forward to each session every week.

Speak about it

A sermon series can set the ground and help a church think a bit about stories. It can also help people to start conversations over coffee and before they go home. A church in conversation tends to be a healthy and happy church.

You can talk about how God invites us to take part in the big story and that our small stories matter to him. People tend to respond positively to this link between narratives and it is a helpful way of showing how our own lives matter.

We can speak about the incarnational God who cares about our ordinary everyday lives, because he lived a life like that as well – working in his father's business, looking after his brothers and sisters, having friends. Jesus would have had a very ordinary story to tell about his first thirty years. If he had come to a group, his early life story would have been normal and unremarkable perhaps – except for his birth. But he wouldn't have remembered this.

This time on Monday

Many churches are aware of the disconnect between life and church. Some of them have started regular sessions of This Time on Monday. The idea is to ask someone to come up during the service and be interviewed about their work and life, what they will be doing and how their faith helps them or makes things difficult.

It can be tremendously interesting to hear about people's weekday life. Listening to these stories is a useful way of asking questions about how God works in the everyday and some of the challenges of being a Christian in today's world. We get to hear about the ethical issues and the times when being a Christian can confront us with dilemmas about what to do and how to do it.

This makes a strong point that church is not just for Sunday – and nor is God, for that matter. It also helps us to see those in our fellowship in a more complete way. When we know something about a person's work or daily life and the joys and struggles of that, then we begin to have a deeper sense of who they are. This also helps us to think about our own everyday lives and the impact of God.

In terms of evangelism, these stories can be very strong. They help people to see the impact of God day-to-day and to see the faith as more than simply a set of ideas. A lawyer talking about why their job matters, a teacher reflecting on how precious the profession is – these things are exceptionally thought-provoking.

When we hear people talk about the things they love and what motivates them, we begin to marvel at the beauty of life and God's part in it.

Encouraging the voiceless

These segments are opportunities for a church to allow voice to those whose stories are not normally heard. In a north London church, the vicar encouraged those who were on the margins, or who had been on the margins, to speak and explain their lives and their struggles.

Sometimes they were testimonies of God's work in a life, at others they were raw stories of hurt and anguish. The end result was that the church began to really understand more about just who was coming along on a Sunday and to realize something of the complexities of folks' experience.

One person, who had come over as a smuggled refugee, spoke about her life. A person who had a terminal diagnosis of cancer shared his story. A young person shared about problems at school.

Art and keep-a-memory

At our memory café we became aware that people were losing their memories, and this caused tremendous grief to all concerned. We collect memories from people – with their permission. We then aim to take a portrait picture of each of those who have donated a memory and keep the memory in a sealed envelope pasted to the back of the picture.

This art is a treasury that celebrated memories that would otherwise be lost.

Remembrance group

Why not set up a remembrance group? We run one every week. People come to have the ubiquitous tea and coffee and cake and then we discuss different aspects of life. Their first day at work. How they met their partner. Favourite sporting event they attended. Old shops. What it was like going to the dog track or speedway. Well-known local characters who have died.

Shared remembrance is a strong way of building community. It is a way of combating loneliness. It is also a great deal of fun. Some sessions, all you can hear from the room is laughter and the occasional burst of song.

This can be combined with a short Bible study and the singing of a hymn. Both of these cement the idea that God is in our past, present and future. It also tends to help people to hang on to their memories for a little longer.

Some very deep questions often come up at these groups – especially about loss and death.

People wonder what will happen after their death. They mourn the loss of so many friends. They speak about loneliness and loss. It can be tough to feel that you are nearly the last of your friends still standing. People wonder what will happen to them, and they wish their friends and loved ones were still around them. This kind of elders' loneliness is often ignored and rarely acknowledged.

This takes careful pastoral handling and some solid doctrine – but it can be a very good space to discuss people's anxieties and the hope that we share of eternity with God. When we get to discuss the sure and certain hope of eternity with God people do really open up about their insecurities and fears.

Inter-generational sessions

A story doesn't count as a story if we have no one to tell it to. Couple this with the way the old and the young bond so well and you get intergenerational storytelling.

We combine our elders' group with visits from our nursery. The children listen wide-eyed as our older folk tell stories of what it was like when they were young. Both young and old and the youngsters' parents benefit hugely from this kind of group.

There is wonderful scope here to involve people from different ethnicities and faiths. There are tremendous stories to be had from people who have made their homes in the UK.

We sometimes welcome pupils from a local school who come to listen and to talk to our elders. Our older folk love it when the youngsters come along and the young people love talking to older people. The subject of the war sometimes comes up and this can be very touching indeed.

Creative writing

Many people, especially when they are older, would like to write their life story down. Sometimes they lack confidence in their writing or feel that people would not be interested in reading the story. They often feel that time is pressing in on them and they want to leave behind something of their lives and all that has happened. The letter-writing generation is particularly good at *writing* things and we can use this inherent skill as part of this activity. Older folk often have high language skills and their writing is something of beauty.

So we can encourage people to start their story and to write down the things in their lives that have mattered to them. Each week they can write one chapter or part of the story. Perhaps about the time they were evacuated, or their wedding day, or what their first day in England was like (probably cold and rainy!). There is an unlimited stock of subjects for remembrance and some of the most unlikely can generate great discussions – favourite old-style sweets often cause a great deal of controversy.

It is relatively easy to put together books of remembrances with photos and words. There are plenty of places on the internet that provide templates and printing resources.

These living life stories can be a tremendous blessing to our elders' families and a treasure that can be left to them and to the church family.

When people have done some writing, encourage them to read it out to the group. It can be a great source of discussion and encouragement. You can also print out some stories and put them on a noticeboard, and of course, with permission, people can record their stories.

Steve Morris can be contacted at:
Twitter: @SteveMorris214
Website: stevemorrisauthor.com

Notes

[1] Frederick Buechner, *Secrets in the Dark* (San Francisco, CA: HarperSanFrancisco, 2006).

[2] John Donne, *Devotions*, Meditations 17. http://www.online-literature.com (accessed 19 August 2019).

1 First Word

[1] Alister McGrath, *Narrative Apologetics: Sharing the Relevance, Joy, and Wonder of the Christian Faith* (Grand Rapids, MI: Baker, 2019), p. 8.

[2] Ray Bradbury, *Fahrenheit 451* (New York: Ballantine Books, 1991).

[3] Florian Illies, trans. Shaun Whiteside and Jamie Lee Searle, *1913: The Year Before the Storm* (London: Clerkenwell, 2014).

[4] Kazuo Ishiguro, *Never Let Me Go* (London: Faber & Faber, 2006).

2 I Fell in Love with Stories – And Then Forgot How to Listen

[1] J.R.R. Tolkien, *The Lord of the Rings* (London: Harper-Collins, 2014).

[2] John Osborne, *Look Back in Anger* (London: Faber and Faber, 1956).

3 Sunday Evening Starts the Journey

[1] Florian Henckel von Donnersmarck, Max Wiedemann and Quirin Berg, *The Lives of Others* (DVD) (Germany: Buena Vista International, 2006).

[2] While the original source is disputed, the earliest publication of this quote can be found in Ian Maclaren, *The Homely Virtues* (London: Hodder & Stoughton, 1904).

[3] John Yorke, *Into the Woods: How Stories Work and Why We Tell Them* (London: Penguin Books, 2013).

[4] Jonathan Gottschall, *The Storytelling Animal: How Stories Make Us Human* (New York: Mariner Books, 2013).

[5] Ibid.

4 The Funeral Before the Funeral

[1] Wendelin Maria Mayer (OSB, *St. Benedict's Manual: A Complete Prayer Book for All Devoted Children of St. Benedict, Patriarch of Monks, and for All Ardent Reverers of His Order* (Regensburg: Fr. Pustet, 1880).

5 The Stories That Set Us Free

[1] Phone interview.

[2] Dietrich Bonhoeffer, *Life Together: The Classic Exploration of Christian Community* (New York: Harper & Row, 1954).

[3] See John 8:32.

[4] See John 4.

[5] Hosanna Poetry and G. Johnson (10 March 2017),
     https://www.youtube.com/watch?v=cxH_DtCuL1k
     (accessed 31.10.18).

[6] See John 10:10, TLB.

[7] Vaughan S. Roberts, *The Power of Story to Change a
     Church* (Cambridge: Grove Books, 2017).

[8] Ruth 1:20.

[9] Judges 11.

6 Jesus and Stories

[1] Philip Yancey, *What's So Amazing About Grace?* (Grand
     Rapids, MI: Zondervan, 2008), p. 11.

[2] Mark 5:34.

[3] Mark 10:21.

7 Jesus the Storyteller

[1] Luke 10:29.

8 What Storytellers Teach Us

[1] Pádraig Ó Tuama, *In the Shelter: Finding a Home in the
     World* (London: Hodder & Stoughton, 2016), p. 127.

2   Buechner, *Secrets in the Dark*.

3   Frank Kermode, *The Sense of An Ending: Studies in the Theory of Fiction with a New Epilogue* (Oxford: Oxford University Press, 2000).

4   https://www.bbc.co.uk/programmes/b097bcv3 (accessed 19.8.19).

5   Matthew 20:16.

6   See Acts 15.

7   See 2 Timothy 4:11.

9 Paul Tells His Story – And Ditches the Theology

1   See 1 Timothy 1:15.

10 Telling Stories in Emergency Situations

1   Roly Bain, *Playing the Fool* (Norwich: Canterbury Press, 2001).

2   G.K. Chesterton, *Orthodoxy* (London: Aeterna Press, 2015).

11 Who Gets to Tell Their Story?

1   Chris Armstrong, *Medieval Wisdom for Modern Christians: Finding Authentic Faith in a Forgotten Age* (Ada, MI: Brazos Press, 2016).

[2] See Matthew 5:3–10.
[3] See John 11:35.
[4] See John 14:6.
[5] See Matthew 19:30.
[6] Matthew 6:10.

12 The Maître d' and the Gucci Shoes

[1] See Matthew 22:8–10.

14 The Playwright and the Schoolboy

[1] This chapter was first published in the Christmas edition of *The Spectator* 2018.

15 Holy Cow

[1] J. Steffen, *Resurgence*, January/February 1995.
[2] Luke 23:34.

16 The Poet and the Asylum Seekers

[1] All quotes from interview with the poet January 2019.
[2] Caroline Smith, *The Immigration Handbook* (Bridgend: Seren Books, 2016). From *The Immigration Handbook*, with kind permission of Seren Books.

17 A Church Changed by Stories

[1] See Matthew 27:46.
[2] Jean Vanier, *Becoming Human* (Mahwah, NJ: Paulist Press, 2008), p. 25.

18 Stories and Prayer

[1] Samuel Wells, https://www.christiancentury.org/article/2014-04/different-way-pray (accessed 6.11.18). See also his book *A Nazareth Manifesto*, chapter 16 (Oxford: Wiley-Blackwell, 2015).
[2] Wells, *A Nazareth Manifesto*.
[3] Ben Quash, *Abiding: The Archbishop of Canterbury's Lent Book 2013* (London: Bloomsbury Continuum, 2012).

19 The Church That Forgot Itself

[1] Roberts, *The Power of Story to Change a Church*, p. 4.
[2] Kenneth E. Bailey, *Poet and Peasant and Through Peasant Eyes* (Grand Rapids, MI: Eerdmans, 1983) pp. 31–2.
[3] See Psalm 95:7.

20 Last Word

[1] C.S. Lewis, *The Weight of Glory: A Collection of Lewis' Most Moving Addresses* (London: HarperCollins, 2013).
[2] THE LAST BATTLE by CS Lewis © copyright CS Lewis Pte Ltd 1956. Used with permission.
[3] Genesis 1:3.

Finding Our Voice

*Unsung lives from the Bible
resonating with stories from today*

Jeannie Kendall

The Bible is full of stories of people facing issues that are
still surprisingly relevant today. Within its pages, people
have wrestled with problems such as living with depression,
losing a child, overcoming shame, and searching for
meaning. Yet these are not always the stories of the well-
known heroes of faith, but those of people whose names are
not even recorded.

Jeannie Kendall brings these unnamed people to vibrant life.
Their experiences are then mirrored by a relevant testimony
from someone dealing with a similar situation today.

Finding Our Voice masterfully connects the past with the
present day, encouraging us to identify with the characters'
stories, and giving us hope that, whatever the circumstances,
we are all 'known to God'.

978-1-78893-037-6

God Conversations

*Stories of how God speaks and
what happens when we listen*

Tania Harris

Stories of God talking to his people abound throughout the
Bible, but we usually only get the highlights. We read: 'God
said "Go to Egypt,"' and then, 'Mary and Joseph left for
Egypt.' We're not told how God spoke, how they knew it
was him, or how they decided to act on what they'd heard.

In *God Conversations*, international speaker and pastor
Tania Harris shares insights from her own story of learning
to hear God's voice. You'll get to eavesdrop on some
contemporary conversations with God in the light of his
communication with the ancients. Part memoir, part
teaching, this unique and creative collection will help you to
recognize God's voice when he speaks and what happens
when you do.

978-1-78078-188-4

Mission in Marginal Places

The Stories

Paul Cloke & Mike Pears (Eds)

The Mission in Marginal Places book series aims to provoke new understandings about how to respond to a very basic question: how might Christians respond to the Spirit's invitation to participate in God's love for the world, and especially in places of suffering and healing, of reconciliation and justice?

The third book, *The Stories*, is an exploration of the processes and practices of 'storying' mission; of listening to others and then telling appropriate stories about interconnected lives.

978-1-78078-185-3

Overflow

Learning from the inspirational resource church of Antioch in the book of Acts

Matthew Porter

Birthed out of The Belfrey, York's call to overflow with the presence and power of God into their locality and region with all the resources God gives, Matthew Porter shares stories of what they have been learning and how this may help the church to reach out in mission and see many come to Christ.

Overflow describes characteristics, structures and strategies that any community of Christ-followers desiring to reach out beyond themselves can adopt. Questions are included at the end of each chapter, with some for individual application and some to help start activating gifts in others.

Discover the God of overflow, who invites us to give away what he gives, and be encouraged to make steps to become a church of overflow, spilling out with the good news of Christ.

978-1-78893-125-0

Infused with Life

*Exploring God's gift of rest in
a world of busyness*

Andy Percey

In a stressful, task-orientated life, we know the importance of
rest, but it is too often pushed out of our busy schedules.

Join Andy Percey as he reveals that rest is actually God's good
gift to us, provided for us to experience a balance in our lives
that isn't just about rest as recovery, but rest as harmony with
our Creator and the world he has made.

By learning to practise life-giving rhythms of rest, we can be
infused with the very best of the life God freely gives us.

978-1-78893-065-9

Face to Face

*Life lessons from Moses –
exploring intimacy with God*

Jen Baker

God longs for us to personally experience more of him, but so often we refuse or feel unable to draw close to him. Even the great hero of faith Moses hid his face from God, yet was eventually transformed into someone who spoke face to face with him.

Jen Baker explores Moses' life to see how he was able to move from hiddenness to holiness and encourages us to follow his example. Interwoven with personal testimony, Jen gently challenges and shows us how to move out of the shadows into the light of God's love.

Whether you feel distant from God or want to deepen your relationship with him, *Face to Face* will help encourage you to experience God in a new and powerful way.

978-1-78893-056-7

Authentic

We trust you enjoyed reading this book
from Authentic. If you want to be
informed of any new titles from this author
and other releases you can sign up to the
Authentic newsletter by scanning below:

Online:
authenticmedia.co.uk

Follow us: